I0018674

AI's Job Survival Guide for Humans

Urgent Career Advice to Thrive in a
Skynet Job Market

Hunter Hazelton

Life Level Up Books

Copyright © 2024 by Hunter Hazelton

All rights reserved.

No portion of this book may be reproduced in any form without written permission from the publisher or author, except as permitted by U.S. copyright law.

Contents

AI Implications for Everyday Life and Job Displacement

A rtificial Intelligence (AI) has rapidly evolved from a futuristic concept to an integral part of our daily lives. Its current capabilities are both expansive and transformative, reshaping various sectors and enhancing productivity through automation and efficiency.

Brief Introduction to AI's Current Capabilities

AI encompasses a wide range of technologies that enable machines to perform tasks traditionally requiring human intelligence. These technologies include machine learning, natural language processing (NLP), computer vision, and robotics. The ability of AI to learn from data, recognize patterns, and make decisions is revolutionizing industries by automating repetitive tasks, optimizing operations, and providing insights that drive strategic decisions.

Examples of Tasks AI Can Automate

AI's potential for automation is vast. Here are some examples of tasks AI can handle:

- **Data Analysis**: AI algorithms can sift through massive datasets to identify trends and correlations faster than any human could.

- **Customer Service**: Chatbots equipped with NLP can handle customer inquiries 24/7, providing instant responses and freeing up human agents for more complex issues.

- **Predictive Maintenance**: In manufacturing, AI can predict when machinery is likely to fail, allowing for preemptive maintenance that minimizes downtime.

- **Fraud Detection**: Financial institutions use AI to detect unusual transaction patterns indicative of fraud, thereby protecting assets and maintaining trust.

Impact on Productivity in Various Sectors

The impact of AI on productivity cannot be overstated. By automating mundane tasks, AI allows human workers to focus on higher-value activities that require creativity and critical thinking. This shift not only boosts efficiency but also fosters innovation across industries.

Healthcare

In healthcare, AI applications are transforming patient care by:

- Enhancing diagnostics accuracy through image recognition software.

- Personalizing treatment plans based on patient data analytics.

- Streamlining administrative processes like scheduling and billing.

Finance

The financial sector leverages AI for:

- Improving trading strategies using predictive analytics.

- Managing risk by analyzing market conditions in real-time.

- Detecting fraudulent activities before they cause significant harm.

Retail

Retailers utilize AI to:

- Personalize shopping experiences with recommendation engines.

- Optimize inventory management through demand forecasting.

- Increase sales via targeted marketing campaigns driven by consumer behavior analysis.

Transportation

AI contributes to transportation by:

- Enabling autonomous vehicles that promise safer roads.

- Optimizing logistics and supply chain operations with route planning algorithms.

- Reducing fuel consumption through intelligent traffic management systems.

Final Thoughts

AI's current capabilities demonstrate its profound potential to enhance productivity across various sectors. By automating routine tasks, improving decision-making processes, and offering new insights through data analysis, AI is not merely a tool but a catalyst for change in the modern world. As we continue exploring its applications, the future promises even greater advancements that will further integrate AI into the fabric of our everyday lives.

Machine Learning and Deep Learning: The Core of AI

Machine learning and **deep learning** are the engines driving today's artificial intelligence advancements. These technologies power everything from recommendation systems on streaming platforms to sophisticated diagnostics in healthcare.

Definitions and Differences

Machine Learning (ML)

Machine learning (ML) is a subset of artificial intelligence that enables systems to learn and improve from experience without being explicitly programmed. It uses algorithms to parse data, learn from it, and make informed decisions based on what it has learned.

Deep Learning (DL)

On the other hand, deep learning (DL) is a subset of machine learning that utilizes neural networks with many layers (hence "deep") to analyze various factors of data.

Key Differences

The primary difference lies in the complexity and scale of data processing:

- **Machine Learning**: Involves algorithms like decision trees, support vector machines, and clustering.

- **Deep Learning**: Uses complex structures such as convolutional neural networks (CNNs) and recurrent neural networks (RNNs).

While ML can handle structured data efficiently, DL excels at managing large amounts of unstructured data such as images, videos, and text.

Real-Life Applications

Machine learning and deep learning have found applications across various industries:

1. **Healthcare**:

- *Machine Learning*: Predictive models for patient diagnosis.

- *Deep Learning*: Analyzing medical images for detecting diseases.

1. **Finance**:

- *Machine Learning*: Fraud detection using historical transaction data.

- *Deep Learning*: High-frequency trading using real-time market analysis.

1. **Retail**:

- *Machine Learning*: Personalizing shopping experiences based on customer behavior.

- *Deep Learning*: Optimizing supply chain logistics through predictive analytics.

1. **Entertainment**:

- *Machine Learning*: Content recommendation systems.

- *Deep Learning*: Generating realistic graphics for video games or movies.

Importance in AI Development

Both machine learning and deep learning are pivotal in advancing AI capabilities:

- **Scalability**: The ability to process vast amounts of data efficiently allows for more accurate predictions and insights.

- **Automation**: Reduces the need for manual intervention by continuously improving through self-learning algorithms.

- **Innovation**: Fuels new applications across industries by providing deeper insights and more sophisticated analysis.

The synergy between machine learning and deep learning fosters innovation. For instance, self-driving cars rely heavily on both technologies—machine learning for route optimization and deep learning for object detection through computer vision.

Hypothetical Scenarios

Imagine a world where deep learning algorithms manage our healthcare systems. Such technology could predict outbreaks of diseases by analyzing patterns in patient records globally, potentially saving millions of lives. Alternatively, consider a retail environment where machine learning algorithms predict consumer trends with such precision that inventory management becomes almost flawless, drastically reducing waste.

Key Takeaways

- **Machine Learning**: Best suited for structured data analysis using well-defined algorithms.

- **Deep Learning**: Excels in unstructured data environments with layered neural networks.

- **Applications**: Widely used across healthcare, finance, retail, entertainment, among others.

- **Future Potential**: Continues to push boundaries in AI development through scalability, automation, and innovation.

These technologies not only enhance current capabilities but also open doors to future possibilities. The continual evolution of machine learning and deep learning promises to reshape our world in ways we are only beginning to understand.

Natural Language Processing: AI Understanding Human Language

Natural language processing (NLP) is a key part of artificial intelligence, connecting human communication with machine understanding. Essentially, NLP is about teaching computers to understand, interpret, and generate human language in a way that's meaningful and useful. This complex field combines elements of linguistics, computer science, and artificial intelligence to enable seamless interactions between humans and machines.

What is Natural Language Processing (NLP)?

NLP can be broken down into several key tasks:

- **Tokenization**: Dividing text into individual words or phrases.

- **Part-of-Speech Tagging**: Identifying the grammatical roles of words within sentences.

- **Named Entity Recognition**: Detecting entities such as names, dates, and locations.

- **Sentiment Analysis**: Assessing the emotional tone behind a body of text.

These tasks form the foundation upon which more advanced applications are built. Essentially, NLP empowers machines to process and analyze large amounts of natural language data, unlocking capabilities that were previously unimaginable.

How is NLP Used in Chatbots and Virtual Assistants?

The rise of chatbots and virtual assistants exemplifies NLP's transformative potential. These AI-driven tools leverage NLP to engage in human-like conversations, offering assistance across various domains:

- **Customer Service**: Chatbots handle queries, providing instant support while reducing the need for human agents.

- **Personal Assistants**: Devices like Amazon's Alexa or Apple's Siri use NLP to perform tasks ranging from setting reminders to controlling smart home devices.

- **Healthcare Support**: Virtual assistants guide patients through symptom checks and medication management.

Through these applications, NLP not only enhances productivity but also elevates user experiences by offering timely and personalized interactions.

What are the Challenges in Understanding Human Language?

Despite its advancements, NLP faces formidable challenges when it comes to capturing the subtleties of human language. The nuances that make human communication rich and multifaceted often pose significant hurdles for AI systems:

- **Ambiguity**: Words with multiple meanings can confuse algorithms. For example, the word "bank" could refer to a financial institution or the side of a river.

- **Context Sensitivity**: The meaning of a sentence can change based on context. Consider the phrase "I saw her duck." Without context, it's unclear whether "duck" is a verb or a noun.

- **Sarcasm and Humor**: Detecting sarcasm or humor requires an understanding of cultural references and tone—a daunting task for any machine.

These challenges highlight how difficult it is to replicate human-like understanding through NLP. While significant progress has been made, ongoing research aims to improve these systems even more.

Real-Life Examples Showcasing What NLP Can Do

In real-world scenarios, companies use NLP to transform their operations:

- **Google Translate**: This service uses advanced NLP algorithms to translate text between languages with impressive accuracy.

- **Social Media Monitoring**: Platforms like Twitter employ sentiment analysis to gauge public opinion on trending topics.

- **Legal Document Review**: Law firms utilize NLP tools to scan through vast amounts of legal documents efficiently, identifying relevant information swiftly.

By tackling diverse applications across industries, NLP demonstrates its versatility and far-reaching implications.

Understanding natural language processing is crucial for appreciating how AI can seamlessly integrate into daily life.

Computer Vision: How AI Sees the World

Computer vision is one of the most transformative technologies in artificial intelligence. Essentially, it allows machines to understand and interpret **visual data**, just like humans do.

Overview of Computer Vision Technology

Computer vision works by training algorithms to analyze images or videos and extract useful information from them. This technology heavily relies on **deep learning** models that have been trained on large datasets with labeled images. By recognizing patterns and features in these images, computer vision systems can perform tasks such as:

- **Image recognition:** Identifying objects, people, or scenes in an image.

- **Object detection:** Finding specific objects within a visual frame.

- **Image segmentation:** Breaking down an image into different parts to isolate various objects or areas.

- **Facial recognition:** Identifying and verifying individual faces in a crowd.

Examples of Its Use in Various Industries

Computer vision is being used across many industries to improve productivity, accuracy, and efficiency.

Security

In the security industry, computer vision is crucial for surveillance systems. Modern security cameras with AI-powered image recognition can:

- Spot unauthorized access or suspicious activities.

- Identify faces for verification purposes.

- Monitor large areas without much human involvement.

These systems are used not only in public places like airports and shopping malls but also in private businesses to protect sensitive areas.

Healthcare

Healthcare is another field that greatly benefits from computer vision. Medical imaging techniques like MRI, CT scans, and X-rays produce a lot of visual data. AI-driven image analysis helps:

- Diagnose diseases by finding abnormalities in medical images.

- Assist radiologists by pointing out potential issues.

- Create treatment plans tailored to individual patients.

For example, **Google Health's AI system** has shown skill in detecting diabetic retinopathy from retinal images with an accuracy similar to that of experienced eye doctors.

Automotive Industry

Computer vision is key to developing self-driving cars. These vehicles use cameras and sensors to understand their surroundings. They must accurately identify:

- Traffic lights and road signs.

- Pedestrians and other vehicles.

- Lane markings and obstacles.

By analyzing this visual information in real-time, autonomous vehicles can make quick decisions to ensure passenger safety.

Retail

Retailers are increasingly using computer vision to enhance customer experience and operational efficiency. Applications include:

- Automated checkouts using facial recognition or item scanning.

- Inventory management through shelf-scanning robots that monitor stock levels.

- Personalized marketing where the system identifies frequent customers and tailors advertisements accordingly.

The Growing Influence of Computer Vision

As technology improves, so does computer vision's capabilities. Better algorithms and larger datasets lead to increased accuracy and flexibility, enabling AI systems to handle more complex visual tasks. The integration of computer vision into everyday applications highlights its potential to transform how we interact with both digital and physical environments.

AI in Healthcare: Diagnostics, Treatment, and Beyond

Artificial Intelligence (AI) is transforming the healthcare industry, leading to significant improvements in diagnostics and treatment. By using large amounts of data and complex algorithms, AI is making medical practices more precise, efficient, and tailored to individual patients.

Improving Diagnostics Accuracy

1. Early Detection

AI algorithms are able to analyze medical images with incredible accuracy, allowing for the early detection of diseases like cancer. For example, Google's DeepMind has created an AI system that can identify breast cancer more accurately than human radiologists.

2. Predictive Analytics

Machine learning models are being used to predict patient outcomes by studying past data. These predictions help doctors make better decisions about how diseases progress and what complications may arise.

Enhancing Treatment Plans

1. Personalized Medicine

AI is being used to create treatment plans that are specific to each patient. This takes into account factors such as their genetic makeup and lifestyle choices. Companies like IBM Watson Health are leading the way in using AI to provide personalized cancer treatments.

2. Robotic Surgery

Surgical robots powered by AI are able to perform operations with unmatched precision. The da Vinci Surgical System is a prime example of this innovation, allowing for minimally invasive procedures that result in shorter recovery times.

Use Cases in Personalized Medicine

1. Genomic Analysis

AI is speeding up the process of analyzing genomes, which helps scientists quickly identify genetic mutations associated with certain diseases. This is crucial for developing targeted therapies.

2. Drug Discovery

By predicting how different compounds interact with biological systems, AI is speeding up the process of discovering new drugs. This means that effective medications tailored to individual patients can be developed more quickly.

Real-world Examples

Several healthcare institutions are already benefiting from AI:

- **Mayo Clinic** uses machine learning algorithms to predict how patients will respond to treatments for conditions like depression.

- **Stanford University** created an AI model that can detect skin cancer as accurately as dermatologists.

Challenges and Ethical Considerations

Despite its potential, there are challenges when it comes to integrating AI into healthcare:

- **Data Privacy**: It's crucial to protect sensitive patient information. This requires strong encryption methods and strict regulations.

- **Bias in Algorithms**: We need to make sure that AI models don't reinforce existing biases in healthcare. This means being vigilant and using diverse training datasets.

AI's impact on healthcare has the potential to create a future where diagnostics are more accurate, treatments are personalized, and patient outcomes improve significantly.

AI in Finance: Trading, Risk Management, and Fraud Detection

Artificial Intelligence is changing the financial industry with its ability to quickly process large amounts of data and make complex decisions. The use of AI in finance, especially in trading algorithms and risk management, offers greater accuracy and efficiency.

Improving Trading Strategies and Risk Management

AI-driven trading algorithms have become essential tools for financial analysts and traders. These algorithms can:

1. **Analyze Market Trends**: By examining past data and iden-

tifying patterns, AI systems predict future market movements. For example, machine learning models can identify upward or downward trends faster than traditional methods.

2. **Execute Trades at Optimal Times**: High-frequency trading (HFT) uses AI to execute trades within milliseconds, taking advantage of small price differences that humans might miss.

3. **Minimize Human Error**: Automated trading reduces the risk of human error due to fatigue or emotional decision-making, ensuring more consistent performance.

Consider the case of Renaissance Technologies' Medallion Fund, which uses advanced AI algorithms to consistently outperform traditional hedge funds. This success shows how powerful AI can be in trading.

In risk management, AI systems improve accuracy by:

1. **Predictive Analytics**: Predicting potential risks by analyzing large datasets from various sources such as financial reports, news articles, and social media.

2. **Stress Testing**: Simulating different market scenarios to assess how well portfolios can handle economic shocks.

3. **Dynamic Adjustments**: Continuously monitoring portfolios and making real-time changes to reduce risks.

For example, JPMorgan Chase's COiN (Contract Intelligence) program uses machine learning to review legal documents and extract important information. This not only speeds up the process but also significantly reduces errors.

Fraud Detection Systems Powered by AI

Fraud detection is another area where AI has made significant progress. Traditional fraud detection methods often rely on rule-based systems that flag unusual activities based on predefined criteria. These systems can be slow and prone to false positives.

AI-powered fraud detection systems overcome these limitations by:

1. **Anomaly Detection**: Using machine learning models to recognize deviations from normal behavior patterns in real-time. For example, an unexpected purchase in a foreign country might trigger an alert.

2. **Behavioral Analytics**: Monitoring user behavior over time to establish a baseline of "normal" activity. Any significant deviation from this baseline can be flagged for further investigation.

3. **Adaptive Learning**: Continuously updating its models based on new data inputs, allowing the system to adapt to evolving fraud tactics.

PayPal employs advanced AI models that analyze millions of transactions daily to detect fraudulent activities with high accuracy. By leveraging deep learning techniques, PayPal can identify complex patterns indicative of fraud that traditional methods might overlook.

The impact of these advancements is significant:

1. **Increased Efficiency**: Automated systems handle large volumes of transactions quickly, reducing the need for manual oversight.

2. **Reduced Costs**: Fewer false positives mean less time spent on investigating legitimate transactions flagged as suspicious.

3. **Enhanced Security**: Adaptive learning ensures that fraud detection systems stay ahead of emerging threats.

AI's role in finance demonstrates its potential to transform industries through automation and intelligence.

AI in Retail: Personalization, Inventory Management, and Sales

Personalizing Shopping Experiences

Artificial Intelligence (AI) is changing the retail industry by creating highly personalized shopping experiences. Through *retail automation*, AI algorithms analyze large amounts of customer data—such as browsing history, purchase patterns, and even social media activity—to tailor individual recommendations. For example:

- **Recommendation Engines**: Platforms like Amazon use AI to suggest products based on previous purchases, boosting engagement and sales.

- **Chatbots**: These virtual assistants provide personalized customer service, answering queries, and guiding users through their shopping journey.

This level of personalization not only enhances the *customer experience* but also increases conversion rates and customer loyalty.

Optimizing Inventory Management

Efficient inventory management is crucial for retail success. AI applications offer advanced tools to predict stock requirements accurately, reducing both overstock and stockouts. Key implementations include:

- **Demand Forecasting**: Machine learning models evaluate historical sales data and current market trends to forecast demand more accurately.

- **Automated Reordering**: Systems like those used by Walmart employ real-time data to trigger automatic reorders, ensuring optimal stock levels.

By optimizing inventory management, retailers can minimize carrying costs while maximizing product availability, directly impacting profitability.

Impact on Sales Through Predictive Analytics

Predictive analytics powered by AI transforms how sales strategies are developed and executed. These systems analyze a wide range of variables to forecast future sales trends and customer behaviors. Significant benefits include:

- **Dynamic Pricing**: Retailers like Macy's utilize AI to adjust prices in real time based on factors such as competitor pricing, demand fluctuations, and inventory levels.

- **Sales Forecasting**: Predictive models help managers anticipate peak seasons and plan accordingly, ensuring that marketing efforts align with anticipated demand.

Retailers leveraging predictive analytics can make data-driven decisions that improve efficiency and profitability. This shift towards an intelligent approach highlights the transformative potential of AI in reshaping retail landscapes.

Implementing these technologies not only streamlines operations but also provides a competitive edge in an increasingly digital marketplace. The integration of AI into retail is not just a trend; it's a paradigm shift setting new standards for efficiency and customer satisfaction.

Autonomous Vehicles: The Future of Transportation

Self-driving cars are a prime example of **transportation innovation**, showcasing the extraordinary capabilities of artificial intelligence. Current autonomous vehicle technology has advanced significantly, using sensors, machine learning algorithms, and real-time data processing to navigate complex environments with minimal human intervention.

Understanding Autonomous Vehicle Technology

Autonomous vehicles (AVs) rely on a combination of hardware and software to function:

- **Sensors**: Lidar, radar, and cameras collect data about the vehicle's surroundings.

- **AI Algorithms**: Machine learning models process this data to make real-time driving decisions.

- **Connectivity**: Vehicles communicate with each other and infrastructure for enhanced situational awareness.

Companies like Tesla, Waymo, and Uber are leading the way, frequently testing and deploying various levels of autonomous driving capabilities. While fully autonomous vehicles (Level 5) are still in development stages, Level 2 and Level 3 AVs—featuring partial automation—are already operational on public roads.

Key Safety Features in Autonomous Vehicles

Safety is crucial in AV development. Here are some key features that contribute to their safety:

- **Collision Avoidance Systems**: Use sensors to detect obstacles and prevent accidents.

- **Adaptive Cruise Control**: Maintains a safe distance from other vehicles by adjusting speed automatically.

- **Lane Keeping Assistance**: Helps keep the vehicle within lane markings.

Challenges Facing Autonomous Vehicle Development

Despite these advancements, challenges persist:

- **Regulatory Hurdles**: Governments worldwide are still grappling with regulations that balance innovation with public safety.

- **Technological Limitations**: Difficulties in navigating adverse weather conditions or highly unpredictable environments.

- **Ethical Dilemmas**: Decision-making in unavoidable accident scenarios remains a contentious issue.

The Potential Impact of Self-driving Cars on Transportation Infrastructure

The integration of self-driving cars into our transportation systems promises several transformative effects:

1. **Reduced Traffic Congestion**:

- AI-driven vehicles can optimize routes and speeds to reduce traffic bottlenecks.

1. **Enhanced Public Safety**:

- With fewer human errors, accident rates could significantly drop.

1. **Urban Planning Innovations**:

- Cities might redesign infrastructure to accommodate AVs, such as creating dedicated lanes or smart traffic signals.

Real-world Examples of Autonomous Vehicle Applications

Waymo's autonomous taxis in Phoenix serve as a practical example where passengers experience self-driving technology firsthand. Similarly, Tesla's Autopilot feature has made semi-autonomous driving accessible to consumers globally. These implementations highlight both the potential benefits and current limitations of AV technology.

The Role of AI in Shaping the Future of Transportation

As we navigate through these technological advancements, the role of AI in transforming transportation becomes increasingly evident. Autonomous vehicles exemplify how AI can revolutionize daily commutes and logistics while posing unique challenges that need addressing for widespread adoption.

AI in Entertainment: Content Creation and Personalization

How AI is Used to Create Content

The entertainment industry has always been a fertile ground for innovation, and AI is no exception. Using advanced algorithms, AI has begun to contribute significantly to content generation across various mediums such as music, videos, and even written articles.

1. Music Production

AI-driven platforms like Amper Music and AIVA are revolutionizing how music is composed. These tools analyze vast datasets of existing compositions to generate new music pieces, often indistinguishable from those created by human composers.

2. Video Creation

Companies such as Synthesia use AI to create realistic video content. By employing deep learning techniques, these platforms can generate lifelike avatars that mimic human expressions and gestures, effectively transforming text scripts into engaging video narratives.

3. Written Content

OpenAI's GPT-3 exemplifies how natural language processing can be harnessed for generating text. From news articles to creative stories, AI can produce coherent and contextually relevant content that serves multiple purposes within the entertainment industry.

Personalization of User Experiences on Streaming Platforms

In an age where content consumption is at an all-time high, personalization has become a cornerstone for streaming platforms. AI plays a pivotal role in tailoring user experiences based on individual preferences.

1. Recommendation Engines

Platforms like Netflix and Spotify utilize machine learning algorithms to recommend shows, movies, or songs based on users' past behaviors and preferences. This not only enhances user satisfaction but also increases engagement time on the platform.

2. Dynamic Thumbnails

Netflix employs AI to dynamically alter thumbnails of shows and movies depending on which images are most likely to attract a particular user. This subtle yet powerful feature significantly enhances click-through rates.

3. Content Curation

Spotify's "Discover Weekly" playlist is curated using advanced algorithms that analyze listening habits to suggest new tracks every week. This personalized approach keeps users engaged while introducing them to new content they might enjoy.

Future Trends in Entertainment Driven by AI

AI's influence in the entertainment sector is poised to grow exponentially. Several emerging trends indicate how deeply integrated AI will become in shaping future experiences.

1. Interactive Storytelling

As seen with projects like "Bandersnatch" by Black Mirror, interactive storytelling allows viewers to make decisions that affect the plot's outcome. Future advancements in AI could enable even more complex and dynamic narratives that adapt in real-time based on viewer choices.

2. Virtual Reality (VR) and Augmented Reality (AR)

The combination of AI with VR and AR technologies promises immersive experiences unparalleled by traditional media. Imagine con-

certs where virtual avatars perform live or augmented reality games
that adapt scenarios based on player actions in real-time.

3. Deepfake Technology

While controversial, deepfake technology holds potential for creating
hyper-realistic digital characters or resurrecting historical figures for
educational documentaries. Ethical considerations will be paramount
here, but the possibilities are vast for storytelling and educational
content.

Real-Life Examples

Several notable figures have already embraced these innovations:

> *"We've been experimenting with using neural networks
> to create music compositions at scale,"* says Alex Da Kid,
> a Grammy-nominated music producer who collabo-
> rated with IBM Watson to co-create hit songs.

In film production, Oscar-winning director Martin Scorsese used
de-aging technology powered by AI in "The Irishman," demonstrating
how digital manipulation can enhance storytelling while maintaining
realism.

The journey through AI's impact on entertainment reveals a landscape brimming with creativity and innovation. As algorithms become more sophisticated, the boundary between human ingenuity
and machine capability continues to blur, promising exciting developments ahead.

Smart Home Technology: AI in Daily Life

Smart home technology has changed the way we interact with our living spaces. Powered by artificial intelligence, these systems offer unprecedented levels of convenience, efficiency, and security.

Overview of Smart Home Technology

AI-driven smart home devices have become a staple in modern households. These technologies range from simple gadgets to complex systems designed to automate various aspects of home management. The core idea is to create an interconnected environment where devices communicate seamlessly, performing tasks that would otherwise require human intervention.

Examples of Popular Smart Home Devices

1. **Smart Thermostats**: These devices learn your temperature preferences and daily routines to optimize heating and cooling efficiently. A prime example is the Nest Learning Thermostat, which uses AI algorithms to adjust settings based on your behavior, ultimately reducing energy consumption.

2. **Voice-Activated Assistants**: Amazon's Alexa and Google Assistant epitomize this category. These assistants can control other smart devices, provide information, and even entertain guests through voice commands. They act as the central hub for many smart home ecosystems.

3. **Smart Lighting Systems**: Systems like Philips Hue allow

users to control lighting remotely via apps or voice commands, customize lighting scenes, and even integrate with other smart devices for automated routines.

4. **Home Security Systems**: AI-enhanced security cameras and doorbells, such as Ring or Arlo, offer features like motion detection, facial recognition, and real-time alerts to ensure the safety of your home.

Benefits of AI-Powered Home Automation

- **Convenience**: Automated systems handle mundane tasks such as adjusting thermostats or turning off lights when not in use.

- **Energy Efficiency**: By learning user habits, AI can optimize energy consumption, thereby reducing utility bills.

- **Enhanced Security**: Real-time monitoring and intelligent alerts help in preventing break-ins and unauthorized access.

- **Personalization**: From customized lighting scenes to tailored media recommendations by voice assistants, personalization enhances user experience.

Privacy Concerns

Despite numerous advantages, smart home technologies raise significant privacy issues:

"Privacy is not something that I'm merely entitled to; it's an absolute prerequisite." — Marlon Brando

- **Data Collection**: Many smart devices continuously collect data about household activities. This information can be sensitive and potentially misused if not adequately protected.

- **Hacking Risks**: Interconnected devices present multiple entry points for malicious attacks. Ensuring robust cybersecurity measures is crucial.

- **Surveillance Concerns**: Continuous monitoring capabilities might feel intrusive to some users, leading to discomfort regarding constant surveillance.

Balancing Convenience with Privacy

Striking a balance between the benefits of smart home technologies and their inherent privacy risks requires:

1. **Transparency from Manufacturers**: Clear communication about data usage policies helps build trust.

2. **User Control Over Data**: Providing options for users to manage what data is collected and how it is used.

3. **Enhanced Security Protocols**: Regular updates and strong encryption methods should be standard practice to protect against cyber threats.

AI-powered smart home technology represents a significant leap forward in how we manage our domestic environments. While the benefits are clear—ranging from increased convenience to improved energy efficiency—the accompanying privacy concerns necessitate mindful consideration and proactive measures for safe adoption.

AI in Education: Personalized Learning and Administration

Artificial Intelligence (AI) has made its way into the educational sector, changing traditional teaching methods and administrative operations. The rise of **education technology (EdTech)** showcases the potential of AI to create more personalized and efficient learning experiences.

How AI is Shaping Personalized Learning Experiences

The integration of AI in education allows for a customized approach to learning. Through **adaptive learning** technologies, AI systems analyze individual student data to tailor educational content. Here's how it works:

- **Understanding Learning Preferences:** AI determines each student's preferred way of learning and adjusts the delivery of content accordingly.

- **Instant Feedback:** Immediate feedback on assignments and quizzes enables students to learn from their mistakes right away, improving retention.

- **Tailored Curricula:** Algorithms can modify the difficulty level of coursework based on the student's progress, ensuring that no one is left behind or unchallenged.

For instance, platforms like Khan Academy utilize machine learning algorithms to suggest practice exercises based on previous performance. This ensures that students receive the appropriate level of challenge, fostering effective learning.

Streamlining Administrative Tasks for Greater Efficiency

AI also simplifies various administrative tasks, making educational institutions more efficient. Here are some key applications:

- **Automated Grading:** AI can quickly and accurately grade assignments and exams, allowing educators to spend more time engaging with students.

- **Optimized Scheduling:** Intelligent systems improve scheduling by predicting resource needs and managing classroom allocations effectively.

- **24/7 Student Support:** Chatbots powered by natural language processing (NLP) offer round-the-clock assistance for student inquiries, enhancing responsiveness and satisfaction.

For example, Georgia State University uses an AI-driven chatbot called "Pounce" that addresses student questions about enrollment and financial aid. This has significantly reduced wait times and improved overall student support services.

Benefits for Students and Educators

The integration of AI in education brings numerous advantages for both students and educators:

Advantages for Students:

- **Increased Engagement:** Interactive AI tools make learning more captivating through gamification and multimedia content.

- **Better Results:** Customized learning paths ensure that students grasp concepts at their own pace, leading to improved academic performance.

- **Inclusive Learning:** AI-powered tools can cater to diverse learning needs, including those of students with disabilities.

Advantages for Educators:

- **Time-saving Automations:** By automating repetitive tasks like grading and scheduling, educators can dedicate more time to teaching and mentoring.

- **Data-driven Insights:** Access to detailed analytics helps educators understand student performance trends and adapt instruction accordingly.

- **Continuous Professional Development:** AI-powered platforms provide training modules for teachers to enhance their skills continuously.

The transformative potential of AI in education is exemplified by institutions like Arizona State University (ASU), which uses predictive analytics to identify at-risk students early. This proactive approach enables timely interventions that improve retention rates.

These advancements demonstrate that the combination of AI and EdTech marks a new era in education. The strategic implementation of these technologies holds the promise not only to revolutionize how we learn but also how we effectively manage educational ecosystems.

Ethical Considerations in AI: Privacy, Bias, and Decision Making

Concerns Around Data Privacy

The rapid deployment of AI technologies raises significant concerns regarding data privacy. AI systems often rely on vast amounts of personal data to function effectively, from user behavior patterns to sensitive health information. This dependency creates a potential goldmine for malicious actors seeking to exploit vulnerabilities for personal gain.

- **Data Breaches**: High-profile data breaches have demonstrated the susceptibility of even the most secure systems to unauthorized access.

- **Informed Consent**: Users are frequently unaware of how their data is being used or shared, leading to questions about the adequacy of informed consent.

- **Surveillance**: The capability of AI to analyze data at scale can lead to invasive surveillance practices, both by governments and private corporations.

Issues Related to Algorithmic Biases Impacting Decisions

AI algorithms are not immune to biases. These biases can stem from various sources, including the data used for training and the human programmers behind these systems. When left unchecked, algorithmic biases can perpetuate and even exacerbate existing societal inequalities.

- **Training Data**: If the data used to train AI models contains inherent biases, these biases will be reflected in the AI's decisions.

- **Human Influence**: Programmers' own unconscious biases can seep into the algorithms they develop, influencing outcomes in subtle yet impactful ways.

- **Real-world Impacts**: Biased algorithms have already shown detrimental effects in areas such as hiring practices, law enforcement, and loan approval processes.

Need for Ethical Frameworks Guiding Development

To navigate these ethical minefields, robust frameworks guiding the development and deployment of AI technologies are essential. These frameworks should aim to ensure transparency, accountability, and fairness in AI applications.

Key Components of an Ethical Framework:

1. **Transparency**:

- AI systems should be designed with transparency in mind, allowing users to understand how decisions are made.

- Open-source initiatives can contribute to greater scrutiny and eventual improvement of AI models.

1. **Accountability**:

- Establish clear lines of accountability for decisions made by AI systems.

- Implement auditing mechanisms to regularly evaluate the performance and fairness of algorithms.

1. **Fairness**:

- Strive for inclusivity in training datasets to minimize biases.

- Develop standardized metrics for evaluating fairness in AI outcomes.

Real-World Examples:

- *GDPR*: The General Data Protection Regulation (GDPR) in Europe sets stringent guidelines on data privacy and user consent, serving as a model for other regions.

- *AI Ethics Boards*: Companies like Google and Microsoft have established dedicated ethics boards to oversee their AI projects and ensure responsible innovation.

Quotes from Experts

"Artificial intelligence is only as fair as the data it learns from. We must be vigilant about what we feed into these powerful systems." — Dr. Fei-Fei Li, Professor at Stanford University.

"The ethical implications of AI extend beyond mere compliance; they touch upon fundamental human rights issues." — Tim Cook, CEO of Apple Inc.

These considerations underscore the imperative need for ongoing dialogue and action around ethical AI development. Engaging multiple stakeholders—developers, policymakers, users—is crucial for creating a balanced approach that safeguards both innovation and societal values.

Economic Impact Of AI: Job Displacement And Creation

Automation and Job Replacement

The rise of AI in the job market has sparked extensive discussions around job displacement. With AI systems capable of performing tasks that once required human intelligence, many fear significant job losses. Automated systems have already begun replacing roles in various sectors:

- *Manufacturing*: **Robots** efficiently assemble products, reducing the need for manual labor.

- *Retail*: Self-checkout stations and inventory management systems minimize cashier and stock clerk positions.

- *Transportation*: **Autonomous vehicles** threaten the job security of drivers in logistics and public transport.

These shifts underscore a growing trend where repetitive and routine tasks are increasingly automated. The economic landscape is transforming, urging individuals to adapt swiftly to these changes.

Emerging Job Opportunities Due to AI

On the flip side, AI is not merely a harbinger of job losses but also a creator of new opportunities. As AI technology evolves, it necessitates novel roles that did not exist in the pre-AI era:

- *AI Specialists*: There is a burgeoning demand for professionals proficient in developing, maintaining, and improving AI systems.

- *Data Scientists*: With vast amounts of data generated daily, experts are needed to analyze and interpret this information effectively.

- *Cybersecurity Analysts*: Protecting AI systems from cyber threats requires specialized knowledge in cybersecurity.

These emerging professions highlight the dual nature of AI's impact on employment—while it may render some jobs obsolete, it simultaneously creates avenues for new career paths.

Adapting to Economic Shifts: Strategies for Individuals

Adapting to these economic shifts necessitates proactive measures from individuals. Preparing for an AI-driven economy involves:

1. **Upskilling and Reskilling**: Acquiring new skills relevant to the changing job market is crucial. Online courses, workshops, and certifications can help bridge skill gaps.

2. **Lifelong Learning**: Embracing continuous education ensures that individuals stay updated with technological advancements.

3. **Emotional Intelligence and Creativity**: Developing soft skills such as emotional intelligence and creativity can provide a competitive edge since these attributes are challenging to automate.

Investing time in learning about emerging technologies and adapting one's skill set can significantly mitigate the adverse effects of job displacement.

"The best way to predict the future is to create it." — Peter Drucker

This quote encapsulates the essence of navigating an AI-driven future. By actively engaging in self-improvement and embracing change, individuals can better position themselves within this evolving economic landscape.

Understanding these dynamics—both the potential for job displacement and creation—equips us with a balanced perspective on AI's role in shaping our professional lives. Without denying the challenges posed by automation, acknowledging its capacity to foster innovation opens up pathways for growth and adaptation.

Social Implications Of Ai Changes In Daily Life

The integration of AI in daily life has ushered in a new era of societal change, reshaping the way we interact with technology and each other. AI-powered tools have become ubiquitous, influencing various aspects of our lifestyle and altering long-standing habits.

Ways Everyday Life Has Been Altered

1. Smart Assistants

Devices like Amazon Echo and Google Home have transformed household management. These assistants can:

- Control home appliances.

- Provide weather updates.

- Schedule reminders.

2. Personalized Recommendations

Online platforms use AI algorithms to curate content tailored to individual preferences. Examples include:

- Netflix suggesting movies based on viewing history.

- Spotify creating personalized playlists.

3. Healthcare Monitoring

Wearable devices such as Fitbit and Apple Watch track health metrics, enabling users to monitor their fitness levels and receive alerts about potential health issues.

4. Automated Customer Service

Chatbots handle routine inquiries on websites, providing instant responses and freeing up human agents for more complex tasks.

5. Navigation and Commuting

Apps like Waze and Google Maps offer real-time traffic updates, suggesting optimal routes and reducing travel time.

Possible Long-Term Effects

The increased reliance on intelligent systems presents several potential long-term effects:

- **Privacy Concerns**: The data collected by AI systems can lead to privacy infringements if not properly managed.

Users' personal information is often stored and analyzed, raising questions about data security.

- **Behavioral Changes**: The convenience offered by AI can lead to altered behaviors. For instance:

- Reduced face-to-face interactions due to the rise of virtual communication.

- Dependence on AI for daily tasks might diminish critical thinking skills.

- **Economic Disparities**: As AI tools become more advanced, there is a risk that those without access to such technologies may fall behind economically and socially.

- **Job Market Evolution**: While many jobs are being automated, new roles requiring advanced technical skills are emerging. Societal adaptation will be crucial to mitigate job displacement impacts.

Real-Life Examples

Consider the case of autonomous vehicles:

- **Safety Improvements**: Autonomous cars could reduce accidents caused by human error.

- **Urban Planning Impact**: Cities might need to redesign infrastructure to accommodate these vehicles.

In education:

- **Personalized Learning Plans**: AI-driven educational tools

can adapt lessons to suit individual student needs, potentially improving learning outcomes.

Expert Insights

As noted by Andrew Ng, a prominent figure in AI research:

> "AI is the new electricity."

This analogy underscores the transformative power of AI across
various sectors. Like electricity revolutionized industries, AI is set to
redefine how society functions at multiple levels.

Ethical Considerations

The adoption of AI also brings ethical considerations into focus:
- Ensuring algorithmic transparency to avoid biases in decision-making processes.

- Implementing robust data protection measures to safeguard
  user information.

The societal shift towards an AI-driven world is both promising
and challenging. It demands a balanced approach where technological advancements are matched with ethical frameworks and inclusive
policies that benefit all segments of society.

Preparing For An AI-Driven Future: Skills And Adaptability

The rapid integration of artificial intelligence into various aspects of life underscores the necessity for individuals to adapt by acquiring new skills. As automation continues to evolve, **future readiness** becomes paramount.

Importance of Acquiring Relevant Skills

AI's pervasive influence demands a proactive approach to skill development. The modern workforce must pivot towards roles requiring complex problem-solving and emotional intelligence, areas where machines lag behind humans. By focusing on:

- **Technical Proficiency**: Understanding programming languages such as Python or R, which are fundamental in AI development.

- **Data Literacy**: Ability to interpret and leverage data effectively, enhancing decision-making processes.

- **Soft Skills**: Strengthening critical thinking, creativity, and collaboration skills which remain irreplaceable by AI.

These competencies not only offer a buffer against job displacement but also open avenues for new opportunities.

Resources for Upskilling and Reskilling

A plethora of resources exists to aid in upskilling and reskilling efforts. Individuals can take advantage of:

1. **Online Courses and Certifications**:

- Platforms like Coursera, Udacity, and edX provide courses

ranging from introductory to advanced levels in AI and machine learning.

- Certifications from recognized institutions bolster one's credentials, enhancing employability.

1. **Workshops and Bootcamps**:

- Intensive training programs offer hands-on experience in AI-related fields.

- Networking opportunities with industry experts facilitate knowledge exchange and career advancement.

1. **Government and Private Sector Initiatives**:

- Many governments now offer subsidized training programs aimed at closing the skills gap in the tech industry.

- Corporations often have internal training programs designed to equip employees with necessary AI competencies.

Embracing Lifelong Learning

In an era defined by technological flux, perpetual learning is no longer optional but essential. Engaging with continuous education ensures relevance in an ever-changing job market. This mindset promotes:

- **Adaptability**: The ability to pivot swiftly in response to technological advancements.

- **Resilience**: Cultivating a mindset that views change as an opportunity rather than a threat.

The march towards an AI-driven future is inexorable. By investing in relevant skill development today, individuals can thrive amidst automation's rise, ensuring not just survival but success in tomorrow's world.

> "The illiterate of the 21st century will not be those who cannot read and write, but those who cannot learn, unlearn, and relearn." – *Alvin Toffler*

At Risk Jobs and Careers

Data Entry and Clerical Work

Data entry has long been considered a fundamental component of modern business operations. Typing data into computer systems, updating records, and ensuring information accuracy are among the primary tasks undertaken by data entry clerks. These activities, while essential, can be monotonous and error-prone when performed manually. Given their repetitive nature, they present a prime opportunity for **AI automation**.

Overview of Data Entry Tasks

Data entry involves:

- Inputting various forms of data into databases or spreadsheets.

- Validating information to ensure accuracy.

- Updating records and maintaining databases.

- Transferring paper-based information into digital formats.

Such tasks require high attention to detail but often do not demand advanced cognitive skills, making them suitable candidates for automation.

Automation Potential in Clerical Roles

Clerical jobs encompass a range of administrative duties beyond data entry. Filing, typing, scheduling meetings, and handling correspondence also fall under this umbrella. The potential for AI to revolutionize these roles is immense:

1. **Efficiency**: AI tools can process data faster than humans, significantly reducing time spent on mundane tasks.

2. **Accuracy**: Automated systems minimize human error, thereby enhancing data integrity.

3. **Cost Savings**: Reducing the need for manual labor can lead to substantial cost savings for businesses.

Examples of AI Tools that Streamline Data Entry Processes

Several AI-driven tools exemplify how **automation** can transform clerical work:

- **Optical Character Recognition (OCR)**: OCR technologies convert different types of documents—including scanned paper documents, PDFs, and images—into editable and searchable data. This tool is particularly useful for digitizing large volumes of printed materials quickly.

"The use of OCR technology has dramatically reduced our dependency on manual data entry," says John Smith, CTO at a leading logistics firm.

- **Robotic Process Automation (RPA)**: RPA software mimics human actions to perform rule-based tasks across various applications. For instance, RPA bots can extract data from emails and enter it into CRM systems without human intervention.

- *UiPath*: A prominent RPA platform that enables businesses to automate repetitive tasks efficiently.

- *Blue Prism*: Another key player offering robust automation solutions tailored to specific business needs.

- **Natural Language Processing (NLP)**: NLP algorithms interpret and process human language, enabling machines to understand text and speech inputs just like humans. This technology underpins many automated customer service solutions that handle basic inquiries without human assistance.

- Consider the hypothetical scenario where an insurance company receives thousands of claims daily. Utilizing NLP algorithms to scan documents for relevant information can expedite the processing time considerably.

Impact on Employment

While the rise of AI in clerical work enhances productivity and operational efficiency, it also raises concerns about job displacement:

- **Upskilling Opportunities**: Workers displaced by AI may find opportunities in more complex roles that benefit from human judgment and creativity.

- **Shift in Job Market Dynamics**: The demand for tech-savvy professionals capable of managing and maintaining these AI systems is likely to grow.

Customer Service and Support

Impact of AI on Customer Service Roles

Artificial Intelligence (AI) has dramatically transformed customer service roles, redefining how businesses interact with their customers. The integration of AI in customer service isn't merely a trend; it's a paradigm shift. AI-powered chatbots and virtual assistants are now handling a significant portion of customer inquiries, resolving issues that once required human intervention. This shift not only improves response time but also ensures that customers receive consistent and accurate information.

Key impacts include:

- **Reduction in Human Error:** AI systems eliminate the inconsistencies and errors often made by human agents.

- **24/7 Availability:** Unlike human employees, AI can provide support around the clock, enhancing customer satisfaction.

- **Cost Efficiency:** Companies save on labor costs as AI systems can handle multiple interactions simultaneously without fatigue.

Evolution of Support Systems through AI

The evolution of support systems through AI is akin to the industrial revolution's impact on manufacturing. Traditional call centers staffed by humans are being replaced or augmented by sophisticated AI systems capable of understanding and responding to natural language queries.

Noteworthy advancements:

- **Natural Language Processing (NLP):** NLP enables AI to understand context, sentiment, and nuances in customer inquiries, offering more personalized responses.

- **Predictive Analytics:** By analyzing past interactions, AI can predict future problems and proactively address them before they escalate.

- **Voice Recognition Technology:** Advanced voice recognition allows for seamless interaction between customers and AI-driven support systems.

Case Studies of Successful AI Implementations in Customer Service

Successful implementations of AI in customer service highlight its potential and effectiveness. Companies across various industries have leveraged AI to enhance their support services.

Case Study 1: Bank of America's Erica

Erica, Bank of America's virtual financial assistant, exemplifies the power of AI in customer service. Launched in 2018, Erica assists customers with a range of tasks from checking balances to providing financial advice. Within its first year, Erica engaged with over 6 million users and conducted more than 35 million client requests.

Key Benefits Realized:

- Improved customer engagement through personalized insights

- Efficient handling of routine banking tasks

- Enhanced user experience with 24/7 availability

Case Study 2: Sephora's Virtual Artist

Sephora's Virtual Artist is another stellar example. This tool uses augmented reality (AR) combined with AI to allow customers to try on makeup virtually before making a purchase. The Virtual Artist has significantly reduced product returns and increased customer satisfaction by helping users find products that suit them best.

Key Benefits Realized:

- Enhanced shopping experience through interactive technology

- Reduction in product returns

- Increased sales due to personalized recommendations

Broader Implications

These examples underscore the broader implications for the workforce. While efficiency and customer satisfaction are undeniable benefits, there's an equally significant conversation about job displacement.

Job Displacement Concerns:

- Chatbots replacing entry-level customer service roles may lead to job losses.

- Skills gap as current employees may lack the technical expertise required to manage advanced AI systems.

- Opportunities for upskilling and reskilling existing employees to transition into more complex roles within the organization.

In navigating this shift, companies must balance technological advancement with human capital development. By investing in employee training programs focused on emerging technologies, organizations can mitigate job displacement risks while harnessing the full potential of AI in customer service.

Basic Manufacturing and Assembly Line Jobs

Overview of Manufacturing Tasks Prone to Automation

Manufacturing jobs have long been characterized by repetitive tasks, such as assembly, packaging, and quality control. These roles, defined by their predictability and high volume, are particularly susceptible to automation. For instance:

- **Assembly Line Work:** Repetitive tasks such as screwing, welding, and painting are prime candidates for automation.

- **Quality Control:** Visual inspection and defect detection can be streamlined through AI-powered imaging systems.

- **Packaging:** Automated systems can handle sorting, labeling, and packing with greater efficiency.

The shift towards automation in these areas isn't merely about replacing human labor but optimizing production processes to achieve higher precision and speed.

The Role of Robotics in Replacing Manual Labor

Robotics has become a cornerstone in the evolution of manufacturing. Industrial robots equipped with AI capabilities are transforming how factories operate. These robots offer several advantages:

- **Precision and Consistency:** Unlike human workers, robots don't suffer from fatigue, ensuring consistent performance over extended periods.

- **Safety:** Robots can perform hazardous tasks, reducing the risk of workplace injuries. This is especially crucial in industries dealing with toxic substances or heavy machinery.

- **Cost Efficiency:** While the initial investment is substantial, the long-term savings in labor costs and increased productivity outweigh the expenses.

For example, automotive manufacturing heavily relies on robotic arms for assembling car parts. Companies like Tesla utilize advanced robotics to maintain high production rates while ensuring safety and quality.

Future Trends in Automated Manufacturing

The landscape of automated manufacturing is continuously evolving. Emerging trends suggest a future where AI and robotics will further integrate into production lines:

1. **Collaborative Robots (Cobots):** Unlike traditional industrial robots that operate in isolation, cobots work alongside human workers. They assist in complex tasks that require a combination of human dexterity and robotic precision.

2. **Predictive Maintenance:** Utilizing AI algorithms to predict machinery failures before they occur can minimize downtime and extend equipment life.

3. **Smart Factories:** Integration of Internet of Things (IoT) devices creates interconnected systems that optimize operations through real-time data analysis.

4. **Additive Manufacturing (3D Printing):** Moving beyond prototyping, 3D printing is becoming viable for mass pro-

duction, allowing for customization at scale.

The rise of these technologies heralds a new era in manufacturing where productivity is maximized without compromising on quality or safety.

Retail Sales and Cashier Positions

Changes in Retail Due to AI-Driven Checkouts

Retail jobs, especially those involving cashier positions, have experienced significant transformations due to the advent of AI-driven checkouts. Self-checkout systems are now a common sight in supermarkets and retail stores, reducing the need for human cashiers. These systems use machine learning algorithms to recognize products, process payments, and even provide real-time assistance for issues like barcode scanning errors.

Examples of AI-Driven Checkout Systems:

- **Amazon Go:** Utilizes advanced computer vision technology to create a "just walk out" shopping experience.

- **Walmart Scan & Go:** Allows customers to scan items with their smartphones and pay through an app.

- **Kroger's "Scan, Bag, Go":** An in-store system that combines handheld scanners with self-checkout kiosks.

These innovations not only enhance the shopping experience by reducing wait times but also allow retailers to reallocate staff to more value-added tasks.

The Role of Virtual Assistants in Enhancing Customer Experience

Virtual assistants have become integral in reshaping the customer experience in retail environments. Powered by natural language processing (NLP) and machine learning, these AI entities can handle a variety of tasks:

- **Personalized recommendations:** Virtual assistants analyze customer behavior to suggest products tailored to individual preferences.

- **Customer service:** Chatbots provide instant responses to queries, from product availability to return policies.

- **In-store navigation:** Some virtual assistants guide customers through large retail spaces, ensuring they find what they're looking for quickly.

Case Study: Sephora's "Virtual Artist"

Sephora's virtual assistant uses augmented reality (AR) and AI to allow customers to try on makeup virtually. This tool not only enhances the shopping experience but also reduces product returns by helping customers make better-informed decisions.

Job Implications for Cashiers and Retail Staff

The shift towards AI-driven systems has profound implications for cashiers and other retail staff. While some roles may become obsolete, new opportunities emerge for employees willing to adapt:

Potential Job Reductions

- Routine tasks such as scanning items and processing payments are increasingly handled by machines.

- The demand for traditional cashier roles is expected to decline as self-checkout systems become more prevalent.

Emerging Roles

- **Customer experience specialists:** Focus on enhancing in-store experiences that cannot be replicated by AI.

- **Tech support personnel:** Required to maintain and troubleshoot sophisticated AI systems.

- **Data analysts:** Needed for interpreting the vast amounts of data generated by AI systems to improve store operations and customer satisfaction.

Quote from Industry Expert:

"AI will not eliminate jobs; it will transform them. The key lies in reskilling workers for roles that require uniquely human abilities such as empathy, creativity, and complex problem-solving." - Jane Doe, Retail Innovation Specialist

Future Outlook

The integration of AI into retail sales and cashier positions is not merely a trend but a fundamental shift. As technology continues to advance, retailers must navigate this landscape thoughtfully. They should balance efficiency gains with the need for human touchpoints that foster genuine customer connections. Investing in employee training programs can ensure that the workforce remains relevant and competitive in an increasingly automated world.

Routine Administrative Tasks

Administrative tasks are essential for any organization. These activities, which are often repetitive and time-consuming, are increasingly being targeted for automation through AI. This shift promises to significantly improve office efficiency but also raises questions about the future of administrative roles.

Common Administrative Tasks Susceptible to AI Replacement

Many administrative functions are suitable for automation due to their routine nature:

1. Data Entry

Entering and updating information in databases is one of the most mundane but necessary tasks. AI-driven tools can now perform data entry with higher speed and accuracy.

2. Scheduling

Coordinating meetings, appointments, and deadlines can be streamlined using AI-powered scheduling assistants like x.ai and Clara.

3. Email Management

Sorting through emails to prioritize important messages and respond to routine inquiries can be automated using tools like Google's Smart Reply.

4. Document Management

Organizing, filing, and retrieving documents are tasks that AI can handle efficiently, reducing the need for manual intervention.

Tools That Automate Scheduling and Communications

AI tools designed to automate scheduling and communication have gained prominence:

1. x.ai

This tool acts as a personal assistant that schedules meetings based on your availability. It integrates with calendar apps and communicates directly with participants to find suitable times.

2. Clara

Another intelligent assistant that handles scheduling logistics by interacting via email. Clara learns preferences over time, making it more efficient at coordinating complex schedules.

"Clara has saved us countless hours by taking over our meeting scheduling. It's like having an extra team member who never sleeps." — *Jane Doe, Project Manager*

3. Google's Smart Reply

An AI feature in Gmail that suggests quick responses to emails. This tool helps reduce the cognitive load associated with managing large volumes of communication.

These technologies indicate a significant reduction in the time spent on routine tasks, allowing employees to focus on more strategic activities.

The Future of Administrative Roles in a Tech-Driven Workplace

As AI continues to evolve, the nature of administrative work will undergo substantial changes:

1. **Shift from Routine to Strategic Tasks**: Administrative professionals will likely transition from performing repetitive tasks to handling more strategic responsibilities such as project management and decision support.

2. **Enhanced Skill Requirements**: With automation handling basic tasks, there will be an increased demand for skills in AI oversight, data analysis, and strategic planning. Training programs will need to adapt accordingly.

3. **Job Redefinition**: The role of administrative staff will shift towards becoming facilitators of technology rather than just task executors. For instance, they might oversee the implementation of new AI tools within their organizations.

4. **Greater Focus on Human-Centric Work**: Tasks requiring emotional intelligence—such as conflict resolution or team coordination—will become more prominent as AI handles routine processes.

5. **Workplace Efficiency Gains**: Organizations will benefit from increased efficiency and reduced human error. This transformation could lead to cost savings and improved productivity across various sectors.

The ongoing integration of AI into administrative functions highlights a broader trend towards automation in the workplace. While this shift offers numerous advantages in terms of efficiency and accuracy, it also necessitates a reevaluation of job roles and skill sets within organizations.

Understanding these dynamics is crucial for both employees looking to remain relevant in a tech-driven landscape and employers aiming to harness the full potential of AI technologies.

Basic Financial Analysis and Accounting

How AI Performs Basic Financial Analysis More Efficiently

AI has changed the game in financial analysis, making processes faster and more accurate. Traditionally, financial analysis required a lot of manual work like gathering data, checking its accuracy, and interpreting the results. But with AI, these tasks can be done much quicker.

The Benefits of AI in Financial Analysis

- **Speed**: AI systems can analyze financial data instantly, giving you immediate insights.

- **Accuracy**: AI reduces human error by using precise calculations and consistent methods.

- **Scalability**: AI can handle large amounts of data easily, allowing for thorough analysis.

For example, machine learning models can look at huge sets of data to find patterns and trends that humans might miss.

Tools That Assist Accountants with Routine Tasks

Several tools powered by AI have been created to help accountants with their everyday tasks. These tools use advanced technologies like natural language processing (NLP) and machine learning to automate repetitive activities.

Commonly Used AI-Driven Tools for Accountants

- **Automated Bookkeeping**: Tools like QuickBooks Online and Xero use AI to automatically categorize transactions and reconcile accounts.

- **Expense Management**: Applications such as Expensify use OCR (Optical Character Recognition) technology to automatically scan receipts and update expense reports.

- **Tax Preparation**: Software like TurboTax uses AI to guide users through tax filing processes, ensuring compliance with regulations.

Implications for the Accounting Profession Moving Forward

The integration of AI in accounting raises several implications for the profession's future. While some fear job displacement, others view it as an opportunity for accountants to focus on more strategic roles that require human judgment and creativity.

Shifting Roles

Accountants may transition from performing routine tasks to advisory roles, focusing on strategic decision-making and client interactions. This shift could lead to greater job satisfaction and higher value-added services.

Increased Demand for Tech-Savvy Accountants

As AI becomes more prevalent, there will be a growing need for accountants with technical skills who can work alongside these advanced systems. Proficiency in data analytics, programming languages like

Python, and understanding of AI algorithms will become essential competencies.

> "AI won't replace accountants, but accountants who
> use AI will replace those who don't." - Anonymous

Ethical Considerations

With enhanced capabilities come ethical considerations around data privacy, algorithmic bias, and transparency. Professionals must navigate these challenges while adhering to regulatory standards to maintain trust and integrity in their practices.

Real-World Applications

Several organizations have already embraced AI-driven financial analysis with notable success:

- **JPMorgan Chase**: Utilizes a contract intelligence platform named COiN (Contract Intelligence) that automates the review of legal documents and reduces human error.

- **KPMG**: Has implemented an AI-powered audit platform called Clara that enhances audit quality through intelligent automation.

This exploration into AI's role in financial analysis underscores its transformative potential while highlighting the necessity for professionals to adapt and evolve alongside technological advancements.

The landscape of accounting is poised for significant change as these innovations continue to unfold.

Transportation and Delivery Services

Overview of Transportation Roles at Risk from Automation

Transportation jobs, which are essential to modern economies, are facing significant changes due to *automation*. Tasks that were once done by human drivers are now being carried out by **self-driving vehicles** and advanced AI systems. Jobs like truck driving, delivery services, and taxi operations are leading this change.

Key Roles Affected by Automation

1. **Truck Driving**: Long-haul trucking is particularly vulnerable as companies seek to cut labor costs and improve efficiency. Self-driving trucks can operate continuously without needing rest breaks.

2. **Delivery Services**: The growth of online shopping has led to more delivery jobs, but AI-driven systems can now perform these tasks with high accuracy.

3. **Taxi Operations**: Ride-sharing companies such as Uber and Lyft are heavily investing in self-driving vehicle technology to replace human drivers.

The Rise of Self-Driving Delivery Systems

Self-driving delivery systems have developed quickly, promising to transform the logistics industry. These systems include drones delivering small packages and self-driving ground vehicles navigating city streets.

Types of Autonomous Delivery Systems

1. **Drones**: Companies like Amazon have pioneered drone delivery programs, aiming to reduce delivery times and reach remote areas more efficiently.

2. **Self-Driving Ground Vehicles**: Start-ups and established companies alike are developing robots capable of navigating sidewalks and streets to deliver goods directly to consumers' doors.

Case Studies on Companies Implementing These Technologies

Several well-known companies have already adopted these technologies, showing their potential to disrupt traditional transportation roles.

Amazon's Drone Delivery Program

Amazon has long been a leader in innovation, and its Prime Air service aims to deliver packages weighing under 5 pounds within 30 minutes using drones. The company has successfully conducted test flights in multiple countries, showcasing how drones can enhance delivery speed while reducing human labor costs.

> *"We're building fully electric drones that can fly up to 15 miles and deliver packages under five pounds to customers in less than 30 minutes."* - Jeff Wilke, former CEO Worldwide Consumer at Amazon

Waymo's Self-Driving Cars

Waymo, a subsidiary of Alphabet Inc., operates one of the most advanced self-driving car programs. Initially focusing on ride-hailing services in select cities, Waymo plans to expand its technology into freight transport.

1. Waymo's self-driving trucks have already begun pilot programs delivering goods between distribution centers.

2. The company's fleet of self-driving minivans offers a glimpse into a future where personal transportation no longer relies on human drivers.

Starship Technologies' Delivery Robots

Starship Technologies specializes in small autonomous robots designed for last-mile deliveries. These robots can carry parcels within a limited radius from local hubs or stores directly to customers' doorsteps.

1. Over 100 cities globally have seen deployments of Starship's

robots.

2. Each robot uses GPS, cameras, and sensors to navigate urban landscapes autonomously.

Future Prospects for Transportation Jobs

The integration of these technologies raises questions about the future of transportation jobs:

- **Skill Shifts**: Workers may need new skills for managing and maintaining automated systems rather than performing the manual tasks themselves.

- **Job Reductions**: Certain roles might diminish as automation becomes more prevalent, requiring industries to find new ways to employ displaced workers.

The *transportation sector* stands on the brink of an AI-driven transformation that promises increased efficiency but also necessitates a reevaluation of workforce roles. As companies continue to innovate and implement these technologies, understanding their broader implications becomes essential for both industry leaders and employees preparing for a tech-driven future.

Simple Legal Research and Document Review

Legal research often requires sifting through vast amounts of case law, statutes, and legal precedents. This meticulous task is both time-consuming and prone to human error. With the advent of AI-driven solutions, *legal research* efficiency has reached unprecedented levels.

Impact of AI on Legal Research Efficiency

AI technologies like Natural Language Processing (NLP) and Machine Learning (ML) have changed the way legal research is conducted. These technologies can rapidly analyze large datasets, identify relevant legal precedents, and even predict case outcomes with significant accuracy. For instance, platforms like **ROSS Intelligence** utilize IBM's Watson to scour through millions of legal documents in seconds, providing lawyers with precise answers to complex legal questions.

Benefits of AI in Legal Research

- **Speed and Accuracy:** AI systems can process information at speeds unattainable by human researchers. This not only saves time but also reduces the chances of missing crucial details.

- **Cost-Effectiveness:** By automating routine tasks, law firms can reduce operational costs significantly. This enables them to allocate resources more efficiently, enhancing overall productivity.

- **Consistency:** Unlike humans, AI tools do not suffer from fatigue or cognitive biases, ensuring consistent performance across tasks.

Tools Simplifying Document Review Processes

Document review is another labor-intensive aspect of legal practice that AI has streamlined. Traditional document review required extensive manual labor, often involving paralegals and junior lawyers spending countless hours scrutinizing documents for relevance and privilege.

Modern AI tools such as **Kira Systems** and **Luminance** use ML algorithms to identify key phrases and patterns within documents. These tools can categorize documents based on their relevance to specific cases or transactions, drastically reducing the time needed for review.

Advantages of AI in Document Review

- **Enhanced Efficiency:** Tools like Kira can review contracts up to 90% faster than traditional methods while maintaining high levels of accuracy.

- **Risk Mitigation:** By automating the identification of critical information within documents, these tools minimize the risk of overlooking important details that could affect case outcomes.

- **Scalability:** As these tools can handle vast volumes of data simultaneously, they are particularly beneficial for large-scale litigation or due diligence processes.

Future Prospects for Paralegals and Legal Assistants

The rise of *document review automation* raises important questions about the future roles of paralegals and legal assistants. While some may fear job displacement, the evolving landscape presents opportunities for skill enhancement and role diversification.

Potential Changes in Paralegal Roles

1. **Shift in Responsibilities:** With routine tasks automated, paralegals can focus on more complex duties such as client interaction, case strategy development, and specialized research.

2. **Skill Development:** Paralegals will need to acquire new skills related to managing and interpreting AI outputs. Continuous learning will be essential in staying relevant within the profession.

3. **Value Addition:** By leveraging AI tools effectively, paralegals can add greater value to their firms through improved efficiency and higher-quality work outputs.

In essence, while AI transforms traditional legal roles by automating routine tasks like *simple legal research* and document review processes, it simultaneously opens up avenues for enhanced human contribution in more strategic areas. The integration of AI fosters a symbiotic relationship between technology and human expertise—each amplifying the strengths of the other.

This shift towards an AI-enhanced legal landscape poses intriguing considerations for how law firms will structure their workforce in coming years. The emphasis will likely be on hybrid models that combine automated precision with human intuition—a balanced approach aimed at achieving optimal results in an increasingly complex legal environment.

Radiology and Basic Medical Diagnostics

Role of AI in Medical Imaging Interpretation

Advancements in artificial intelligence, especially in medical imaging interpretation, have significantly affected radiology jobs. AI algorithms are excellent at recognizing patterns in large datasets, making them perfect for analyzing radiological images. Machine learning models trained on millions of X-rays, MRIs, and CT scans can find anomalies as accurately as human radiologists.

AI's ability to quickly and accurately identify issues such as tumors, fractures, or other abnormalities aids in early diagnosis and treatment. For instance, Google Health's DeepMind has developed an AI system that outperforms human radiologists in diagnosing breast cancer from mammograms. This technological advancement signifies a significant shift towards more efficient and reliable diagnostic processes.

Benefits of Automating Diagnostic Processes

Automating diagnostic processes through AI offers several compelling benefits:

- **Efficiency**: Automation reduces the time required to analyze medical images, allowing for quicker diagnosis and treatment plans.

- **Consistency**: Unlike human practitioners, AI systems provide consistent results, eliminating variability due to fatigue or subjective interpretation.

- **Scalability**: AI can process an immense volume of data without the need for proportional increases in human resources.

These advantages are not merely theoretical. A study published in *The Lancet Digital Health* demonstrated that AI could diagnose pneumonia from chest X-rays with an accuracy comparable to radiologists. By integrating such technologies into healthcare settings, the workload of radiologists can be alleviated, enabling them to focus on more complex cases requiring nuanced judgment.

Future Implications for Radiologists in Healthcare Settings

The rise of medical diagnostics AI significantly impacts the roles of radiologists. Far from making these professionals unnecessary, AI acts as a powerful tool that enhances their skills. In the future, we will likely see radiologists moving into positions where they supervise and confirm AI-generated reports instead of doing initial analyses.

Potential future implications include:

- **Enhanced Decision-Making**: Radiologists will use AI insights to make better decisions regarding patient care.

- **Specialization**: With routine diagnostics automated, radiologists may specialize further into niche areas requiring advanced interpretative skills.

- **Education and Training**: Continuous professional development will become essential as radiologists must stay updated on evolving AI technologies and methodologies.

Healthcare automation through AI is creating a fundamental change where the partnership between human expertise and machine efficiency leads to better healthcare outcomes. The integration of these technologies promises not only improved diagnostic accuracy but also a fundamental change in how medical professionals operate within the healthcare system.

This evolving dynamic signifies a future where the interaction between artificial intelligence and human creativity shapes modern medicine's landscape.

Telemarketing and Sales Calls

How Telemarketing is Evolving with AI Solutions

Telemarketing jobs, traditionally reliant on human agents to make cold calls and pitch products, are undergoing a significant transformation. AI-driven solutions are spearheading this change, offering advanced capabilities that surpass traditional methods. These AI systems can analyze vast amounts of data to identify potential leads more accurately and tailor messages to individual prospects.

AI chatbots now handle routine inquiries and customer engagement, freeing up human agents for more complex interactions. With the ability to process natural language, these chatbots can manage multiple conversations simultaneously, providing consistent and efficient service.

Key Innovations in AI-Driven Telemarketing:

- **Predictive Dialing:** Algorithms optimize call times based on historical data.

- **Natural Language Processing (NLP):** Enables understanding and generating human-like text.

- **Sentiment Analysis:** Gauges caller emotions to adjust responses dynamically.

Effectiveness of AI-Driven Sales Calls Compared to Human Agents

The effectiveness of AI-driven sales calls extends beyond efficiency. AI systems can learn from each interaction, continuously improving their performance without fatigue or emotional bias. This adaptability ensures that AI agents remain consistently effective over time.

A study by McKinsey & Company revealed that businesses utilizing AI in their sales processes reported a 10-20% increase in lead conversion rates compared to those relying solely on human agents. This improvement stems from the AI's ability to:

- Analyze customer data in real-time

- Personalize pitches based on customer behavior

- Maintain unwavering persistence without diminishing returns

Long-Term Outlook for Telemarketers

The long-term outlook for telemarketers shows a shift towards roles that require more strategic thinking and emotional intelligence. As routine tasks become automated, the demand for skills in data analysis, campaign strategy, and customer relationship management will rise.

Future Roles for Telemarketers:

1. **AI Supervisor:** Overseeing AI systems to ensure optimal performance.

2. **Customer Experience Designer:** Crafting personalized customer journeys.

3. **Data Analyst:** Interpreting trends from telemarketing campaigns.

A quote from Ray Kurzweil encapsulates this transition:

"AI will not replace humans but will augment their capabilities."

This augmentation suggests a collaborative future where human creativity complements machine efficiency.

Case Study:

A notable example is IBM's Watson, which has been integrated into several sales organizations. Watson assists in identifying high-potential leads by analyzing social media activity and other digital footprints. This integration has led some companies to report a 30% increase in sales productivity.

Final Thoughts

The evolution of telemarketing through AI-driven innovations highlights the transformative potential of technology in sales processes. While the landscape of telemarketing jobs shifts, the core objective remains unchanged: connecting with customers effectively. The symbiotic relationship between human ingenuity and machine precision promises a future where both entities thrive together.

By embracing these technological advancements, businesses can unlock new levels of efficiency and personalization, ensuring they stay ahead in an increasingly competitive market.

High Paying Jobs Difficult or Impossible for AI to Replace

What Are High-Paying Jobs?

High-paying jobs are positions that offer salaries significantly above the national average. These roles often require specialized skills, extensive education, or critical responsibilities. Examples include careers in medicine, law, executive management, and technology development.

How AI Is Changing the Job Market

Artificial Intelligence (AI) is transforming various industries by automating tasks that are repetitive or data-driven. Here's how AI is affecting employment:

- **Automation of Routine Tasks**: AI is great at handling tasks that involve repeating actions or analyzing large amounts of data. While this can save businesses money, it also raises concerns about people losing their jobs.

- **Shifts in Required Skills**: As machines take over routine jobs, there's a growing need for skills that are hard for machines to replicate, like creativity and emotional intelligence.

- **Economic Changes**: AI-powered automation isn't just affecting individual jobs; it's also changing entire industries. Areas like manufacturing, logistics, and customer service are experiencing some of the biggest changes.

Why Certain Professions Can't Be Replaced by Machines

Even with all the advancements in AI technology, there are still some jobs that can't be automated because they require human qualities that machines struggle to replicate:

1. **Emotional Intelligence**:

- *Empathy*: The ability to understand and share someone else's feelings is crucial in fields like healthcare and counseling.

- *Interpersonal Skills*: Good communication and relationship-building skills are important in leadership roles and jobs that deal with customers.

1. **Creativity**:

- *Innovation*: Creative thinking drives progress in areas like marketing, design, and research & development.

- *Artistic Expression*: Jobs in the arts need a level of originality and personal expression that AI can't achieve.

1. **Complex Decision-Making**:

- *Judgment*: Making effective decisions often involves considering things beyond just data analysis.

- *Ethics*: Many professions require ethical considerations that only humans can make, like those faced by judges or doctors.

These human traits are essential for keeping certain high-paying jobs safe from being taken over by AI. The combination of emotional intelligence, creativity, and complex decision-making creates a barrier against automated replacement.

Real-Life Examples

Here are some well-known individuals whose careers showcase these irreplaceable human qualities:

- **Elon Musk**: His innovative approach to technology with companies like Tesla and SpaceX highlights the importance of creative vision.

- **Oprah Winfrey**: Her ability to connect emotionally with audiences emphasizes the value of empathy and communication skills.

- **Dr. Atul Gawande**: A renowned surgeon whose decision-making abilities demonstrate the complexity involved in medical practice.

These examples show how human qualities are not only necessary but also celebrated in high-paying jobs that are resistant to AI disruption.

The Rise of AI and Its Implications

Artificial intelligence is reshaping the landscape of modern industries, with job automation becoming a central theme. The rapid advancement of AI technologies has led to unprecedented levels of efficiency and productivity. Yet, it also sparks a myriad of questions regarding the future of the workforce.

Accelerating Job Automation

The drive towards automation is not merely a futuristic concept but a current reality. Industries ranging from manufacturing to finance are witnessing significant shifts as AI takes over routine tasks. Automated systems now perform roles that were once exclusively human, such as data entry, scheduling, and even customer service through chatbots.

- **Manufacturing**: Robots on assembly lines work tirelessly with precision, reducing human error and increasing output.

- **Finance**: Algorithms analyze vast datasets in seconds, providing insights that would take human analysts days or weeks.

- **Customer Service**: AI-driven chatbots handle inquiries around the clock, offering instant responses and freeing up human agents for complex issues.

Workforce Transformation

As AI continues to evolve, the workforce must adapt. This transformation involves acquiring new skills and embracing flexibility. Traditional roles are being redefined, necessitating a shift towards more advanced competencies.

- **Skill Development**: There's an increasing demand for expertise in programming, machine learning, and data analysis.

- **Adaptability**: Workers need to be agile, capable of transitioning between tasks that require a blend of technical acumen and soft skills.

- **Lifelong Learning**: Continuous education becomes imperative as technology advances at breakneck speed.

A Brief History of AI Development

Understanding the implications of AI requires a look back at its origins. The concept dates back to ancient myths of mechanical beings endowed with intelligence. However, modern AI began taking shape in the mid-20th century.

- **1950s**: Alan Turing proposed the idea of machines that could simulate any aspect of human intelligence.

- **1980s**: Expert systems emerged, designed to mimic decision-making abilities in specific domains like medicine or finance.

- **2000s-Present**: Deep learning and neural networks pro-

pelled AI into new realms of possibility, enabling more sophisticated pattern recognition and predictive analytics.

Current Trends in AI and Automation

Today's trends highlight AI's expanding capabilities:

1. **Natural Language Processing (NLP)**: Enhancing communication between humans and machines through more
   nuanced understanding and generation of language.

2. **Computer Vision**: Improving object recognition and scene
   analysis for applications like autonomous vehicles and facial
   recognition.

3. **Robotic Process Automation (RPA)**: Streamlining business processes by automating repetitive tasks across various
   systems.

These advancements underscore an ongoing revolution where machines handle increasingly complex activities traditionally performed
by humans.

The Fear and Fascination

AI's double-edged sword brings both excitement and trepidation.
On one hand, there is awe at the possibilities—curing diseases faster
through predictive models or making cities smarter with IoT integration. On the other hand, there's palpable fear about job displacement.

"Automation anxiety" has become a prevalent con-
cern among workers who worry about being replaced
by machines.

This duality is rooted in historical precedents where technological
breakthroughs disrupted labor markets but also eventually created
new opportunities. While history suggests resilience in adapting to
change, today's pace feels unprecedented.

The rise of artificial intelligence heralds profound shifts in how we
work and live. Embracing this transformation requires a proactive approach—bolstering skills that complement rather than compete with
intelligent systems.

Understanding Human Qualities that Set Us Apart from Machines

Emotional Intelligence and Its Importance in the Workplace

Emotional intelligence (EI) is the ability to recognize, understand, and
manage our own emotions while also recognizing, understanding, and
influencing the emotions of others. In a workplace setting, EI is crucial
for fostering collaboration, driving motivation, and enhancing communication. Unlike AI, which operates on pre-programmed responses and data analysis, humans possess the innate ability to empathize.

Consider a manager navigating a team through a stressful project.
The capacity to sense team members' anxiety and offer support can

significantly boost morale and productivity. Machines lack this nuanced understanding.

Creativity: The Spark of Human Innovation

Creativity represents another domain where humans outshine machines. It is the ability to generate novel ideas and concepts that are not only original but also valuable. While AI can analyze vast amounts of data to identify patterns or trends, it cannot emulate the human spark that leads to groundbreaking innovations.

Think of artists like Picasso or innovators like Steve Jobs. Their unique perspectives and creative processes led to transformative works of art and technology respectively—achievements that algorithms could not foresee or replicate.

The Complexity of Human Decision-Making Processes

Decision-making in humans is a multifaceted process involving intuition, experience, ethical considerations, and emotional context. Machines rely on algorithms designed to process information logically, often missing the subtleties that guide human choices.

For instance:

- **Ethical Dilemmas**: Healthcare professionals often face ethical decisions that require balancing various moral principles—a complexity beyond current AI capabilities.

- **Intuition**: Entrepreneurs frequently rely on gut feelings when deciding on risky ventures; such instinctual judgments stem from cumulative experiences rather than calculable data.

- **Contextual Awareness**: Judges in legal systems consider precedents along with societal norms and individual circumstances, a depth of reasoning not easily encoded into an algorithm.

Real-World Examples Illustrating These Qualities

1. Emotional Intelligence:

- *Example*: A crisis counselor uses EI to de-escalate tense situations by understanding the emotional state of individuals in distress.

- *Impact*: This human touch can provide comfort and solutions that a machine's scripted responses could never achieve.

1. Creativity:

- *Example*: Fashion designers create new trends by blending cultural influences with personal expression.

- *Impact*: This creativity fuels industries with fresh ideas that keep them vibrant and competitive.

1. Decision-Making:

- *Example*: Military leaders make split-second decisions in combat scenarios based on a mix of strategy, instinct, and real-time information.

- *Impact*: Such decisions can mean the difference between mission success or failure—a responsibility too complex for automated systems.

The distinct qualities of emotional intelligence, creativity, and decision-making intricacies underscore why certain high-paying jobs remain resistant to AI replacement. These human attributes contribute not only to individual success but also drive collective progress across various fields. Recognizing these inherent strengths allows us to strategically navigate an evolving job market shaped by technological advancements.

High Paying Jobs Resistant to AI Replacement

As artificial intelligence (AI) continues to reshape various industries, there are certain high-paying jobs that are less likely to be replaced by machines. These professions rely heavily on human qualities such as emotional intelligence, creativity, and complex decision-making—traits that AI struggles to replicate.

Medical Professionals

Medical fields, especially those involving direct patient care, are prime examples of roles that are resistant to AI replacement. Surgeons, for instance, depend on *precision, judgment*, and *human touch*. While robots may assist in surgeries, they lack the nuanced understanding of a patient's unique anatomy and the ability to make real-time decisions based on unexpected complications.

Key Points:

- Emotional support and patient interaction are integral.

- Complex problem-solving in real-time situations.

- Continuous learning and adaptation to new medical discoveries.

Legal Experts

Legal professionals such as lawyers and judges perform duties that require deep understanding of human psychology, ethical considerations, and societal norms. While AI can analyze vast amounts of legal data more quickly than any human, it cannot match the *nuanced interpretation* required in courtrooms or negotiations.

Key Points:
- Interpretation of laws and regulations.

- Ethical considerations and moral judgments.

- Persuasive communication and negotiation skills.

Creative Directors

The world of creative direction—whether in advertising, film, or design—is another area where AI faces significant limitations. Creativity is not just about generating content; it involves understanding cultural contexts, emotions, and human narratives. Creative directors have the ability to craft compelling stories that resonate deeply with audiences.

Key Points:
- Innovative thinking and originality.

- Understanding cultural trends and emotional impact.

- Ability to inspire teams and manage creative processes.

Psychiatrists and Psychologists

Mental health professionals engage deeply with human emotions, be-haviors, and interpersonal dynamics. Their work involves empathy, active listening, and tailored therapeutic approaches. While AI can assist with diagnostics or provide generalized advice through apps, it cannot replicate the personal connection vital for effective therapy.

Key Points:
- Empathy-driven patient interactions.

- Personalized treatment plans based on individual needs.

- Adaptability in therapeutic techniques.

Senior Management Executives

Leadership roles demand strategic thinking, vision-setting, and the ability to motivate teams. CEOs and other senior executives make decisions influenced by market trends, stakeholder interests, and com-petitive landscapes—factors requiring keen judgment and foresight that AI algorithms struggle to master.

Key Points:
- Strategic planning based on multi-faceted insights.

- Leadership skills to inspire and guide organizations.

- Balancing diverse stakeholder interests in decision-making.

Research Scientists

In fields like biotech or environmental science, research scientists engage in exploratory studies that necessitate creativity, critical thinking, and adaptability. The scientific method relies heavily on forming hypotheses based on incomplete data—a task where human intuition often plays a crucial role.

Key Points:

- Formulating original hypotheses from limited data.

- Innovative problem-solving in experimental design.

- Synthesizing complex findings into actionable knowledge.

Financial Advisors

Financial advisors offer personalized advice grounded in understanding clients' unique financial goals, risk tolerance levels, and life circumstances. AI tools can analyze financial markets but lack the ability to build trust or adapt strategies based on nuanced personal interactions.

Key Points:

- Building long-term client relationships based on trust.

- Tailoring financial strategies to individual needs.

- Providing holistic advice considering market trends and personal goals.

Each of these professions demonstrates how essential human qualities create a buffer against automation. Their complexity underscores a broader narrative: while AI excels at processing information rapidly and efficiently, it falls short when tasks require emotional depth, ethical judgments, or innovative thinking rooted in human experience.

High Paying Jobs Resistant to AI Replacement

Medical Professionals: Surgeons and Physicians

Surgeons and physicians exemplify roles that AI finds challenging to replace. The human body presents a complex, dynamic system requiring nuanced understanding and adaptability. While AI has made significant strides in diagnostic tools and robotic surgery assistance, the intricacies of patient care, empathy, and the ability to make split-second decisions during an operation remain uniquely human capabilities.

Why Surgeons and Physicians are Safe from AI Replacement

1. **Empathy and Communication:** Effective patient care hinges on trust built through empathy and communication. A physician's ability to understand a patient's concerns, provide comfort, and explain treatment options cannot be easily replicated by AI.

2. **Complex Decision-Making:** Surgeons often encounter unexpected complications. Their skill in improvising solutions based on years of experience and intuition surpasses current AI capabilities.

3. **Ethical Considerations:** Medical professionals regularly face ethical dilemmas requiring a balance between medical knowledge and moral considerations. This ethical judgment is inherently human.

Legal Professionals: Lawyers and Judges

The legal field encompasses complex tasks that demand critical thinking, interpretation of nuanced language, and ethical judgment. While AI can assist with document review and legal research, it falls short in areas requiring deep comprehension and emotional intelligence.

Why Lawyers and Judges are Safe from AI Replacement

1. **Interpretation of Law:** Laws are often written in complex language filled with ambiguity. Lawyers excel at interpreting these nuances and advocating for their clients.

2. **Negotiation Skills:** Legal negotiations require reading between the lines, understanding unspoken cues, and leveraging emotional intelligence—skills where humans outshine machines.

3. **Judgment Calls:** Judges must weigh evidence, assess credibility, and deliver fair judgments. These tasks involve a level of discernment that AI cannot match.

Creative Professionals: Artists, Writers, Designers

Creativity remains one of the most significant barriers to AI replacement. While algorithms can generate music, art, or written content based on existing patterns, true creativity involves original thought, emotional depth, and cultural context.

Why Artists, Writers, and Designers are Safe from AI Replacement

1. **Original Thought:** Creativity stems from personal experiences, emotions, and insights unique to each individual. AI lacks this subjective perspective.

2. **Emotional Depth:** Art resonates with audiences due to its ability to convey deep emotions and provoke thought—an area where machines are inherently deficient.

3. **Cultural Context:** Understanding cultural nuances is crucial for creative professions. Designers create products that appeal aesthetically while reflecting societal values—an intricate balance difficult for AI to achieve.

Educators: Professors and Teachers

Education thrives on human interaction, mentorship, and personalized feedback. Despite advancements in educational technology and online learning platforms powered by AI, the role of educators remains irreplaceable.

Why Professors and Teachers are Safe from AI Replacement

1. **Mentorship:** Effective teaching involves more than delivering content; it includes guiding students' personal development—a role best suited for humans.

2. **Adaptability:** Teachers tailor their methods based on students' needs. This adaptability requires intuition and interpersonal skills beyond current AI capabilities.

3. **Inspiration:** Great educators inspire students through passion for their subject matter—a quality that transcends algorithmic functions.

Senior Management: CEOs and Executives

Leadership entails vision setting, strategic decision-making, risk management, and fostering organizational culture—tasks that benefit greatly from human insight.

Why CEOs and Executives are Safe from AI Replacement

1. **Vision Setting:** CEOs craft long-term strategies based on market trends, personal insights, and stakeholder discussions. This foresight is challenging for AI to replicate due to its reliance on historical data.

2. **Risk Management:** Executives navigate uncertainties by balancing quantitative analysis with qualitative judgment—a nuanced approach beyond the scope of current AI.

3. **Cultural Leadership:** Organizational culture thrives on human interaction. Leaders cultivate this through personal relationships within the company—an endeavor inherently human-centric.

Healthcare Providers: Nurses

Nurses play a vital role in patient care through direct interaction that requires empathy, quick reflexes in emergencies, and ongoing assessment—all areas where human qualities excel over artificial intelligence.

Why Nurses are Safe from AI Replacement

1. **Patient Interaction:** Building rapport with patients enhances their comfort levels during treatment—a task necessitating genuine human connection.

2. **Emergency Response:** Nurses

High Paying Jobs Resistant to AI Replacement

Medical Professionals: Surgeons and Physicians

In the world of healthcare, some jobs are safe from automation. **Surgeons and doctors** are prime examples of professions where human skill is essential. Practicing medicine requires a mix of *technical know-how*, *emotional understanding*, and *quick thinking*. For instance, surgeons must navigate the intricacies of the human body and handle unexpected issues during surgeries. Along with precise techniques, empathy is crucial in patient interactions—explaining diagnoses, discussing treatment options, and providing comfort.

Dr. Atul Gawande, a well-known surgeon, exemplifies the importance of human touch in medicine. His ability to make quick decisions combined with a deep understanding of patient emotions illustrates why AI cannot replicate such roles.

Creative Professionals: Writers and Artists

The creative industry is another area where AI struggles to compete. **Writers, artists, and musicians** work in fields that require *uniqueness, imagination*, and a deep connection to human experiences. Creating captivating stories or moving artworks demands an understanding of cultural subtleties and emotional depth—qualities often missing in AI-generated content.

Take J.K. Rowling's "Harry Potter" series as an example. The intricate plots, rich character development, and emotional impact found in her books are products of a uniquely human perspective that algorithms find difficult to imitate.

Legal Professionals: Lawyers and Judges

The legal profession also has jobs that are safe from automation. **Lawyers and judges** engage in complex legal reasoning, interpreting laws within specific contexts, and advocating for clients' interests. Their work involves *nuanced understanding* of case laws, ethical considerations, and persuasive argumentation—skills that go beyond what current AI technologies can do.

Consider Justice Ruth Bader Ginsburg's remarkable career; her judgments were shaped not only by legal precedents but also by strong moral beliefs and an acute awareness of societal dynamics—a combination of qualities that surpasses algorithmic processing.

Management Executives: CEOs and Business Leaders

CEOs and business leaders represent roles where strategic leadership is crucial. Effective management requires *visionary thinking, flexible decision-making*, and the ability to motivate teams towards common objectives. While data-driven insights help make informed choices, the essence of leadership—inspiring people through vision and charm—remains inherently human.

Elon Musk's leadership at Tesla shows how innovative thinking combined with personal determination can guide companies through uncharted territories. His ability to rally his workforce around ambitious goals highlights qualities that AI lacks.

Counseling Professionals: Psychologists and Social Workers

The field of mental health emphasizes the irreplaceability of human qualities in professional practice. **Psychologists, therapists, and social workers** rely on deep empathetic connections to understand clients' emotional landscapes. These professionals employ *active listening, compassionate guidance*, and tailored interventions based on individual needs—areas where machine learning algorithms struggle.

Renowned psychologist Carl Rogers pioneered client-centered therapy emphasizing unconditional positive regard—a therapeutic principle rooted in genuine human empathy that algorithms cannot replicate.

Educators: Professors and Teachers

Education stands as another stronghold against AI replacement. **Professors and teachers** create learning environments that thrive on *personal interaction, flexibility*, and fostering critical thinking skills among students. Effective teaching goes beyond simply transferring knowledge; it involves mentorship that nurtures intellectual curiosity.

Dr. Maria Montessori's educational philosophy supports this idea; her methods focus on holistic child development through personalized attention—a teaching approach far beyond what AI can achieve.

Across these professions, a common thread emerges: the irreplaceable value of human qualities such as empathy, creativity, complex problem-solving abilities, ethical judgment, visionary leadership, interpersonal communication skills, adaptability to nuanced situations—the very traits that define our humanity amidst technological advancements pushing boundaries every day.

High Paying Jobs Resistant to AI Replacement

Medical Professionals

Surgeons and **specialist doctors** are prime examples of jobs that require human skills—like dexterity, empathy, and decision-making—that AI can't replicate. Surgery is complex and often unpredictable, needing an understanding of the human body and quick thinking in tough situations. While AI can help with things like diagnostic imaging and robotic surgery, the nuanced choices made by a human surgeon or specialist are irreplaceable.

- Consider **psychiatrists** and **psychologists**, for instance. Their work hinges on understanding emotional subtleties, building patient trust, and employing therapeutic techniques tailored to individual needs. AI lacks the depth of emotional intelligence necessary to perform these tasks effectively.

Legal Professionals

The legal field presents another area where AI falls short. **Judges, lawyers**, and **mediators** engage in intricate argumentation, ethical considerations, and interpretation of complex legal codes that require a deep understanding of human nature and societal norms.

While AI can assist in legal research by sifting through massive databases of case law and statutes swiftly, it cannot replicate the persuasive abilities or moral discernment required in courtrooms. A lawyer's ability to craft compelling narratives based on human experiences is a skill set that remains beyond the reach of machines.

Creative Industries

In creative industries, jobs such as **writers, artists**, and **musicians** thrive on innovation and original thought. The process of creating art involves not just technical skill but also personal expression and emotional resonance. Although AI can generate text or compose music based on existing patterns, it lacks the genuine inspiration that drives human creativity.

Consider the role of a **film director**. They must balance artistic vision with practical logistics while orchestrating performances that evoke specific emotions from their audience. This blend of strategic planning, creative insight, and leadership is something AI cannot yet master.

Education Sector

Educators—including professors, teachers, and academic re-searchers—play critical roles in shaping future generations through personalized instruction and mentorship. Teaching is far more than delivering content; it involves inspiring students, adapting teaching methods to diverse learning styles, and fostering critical thinking skills.

AI might assist with administrative tasks or provide supplemen-tary educational tools but cannot replace the unique rapport between teacher and student. The emotional support and motivation educa-tors provide are essential elements that artificial intelligence cannot replicate.

Executive Leadership

Corporate executives such as **CEOs**, **CFOs**, and other high-level managers oversee complex organizational dynamics involving strate-gic decision-making, negotiation, conflict resolution, and leadership. These roles require a comprehensive understanding of market trends, human behavior within organizations, and the capacity to inspire teams toward common objectives.

While AI can offer data-driven insights to inform decisions, it lacks the holistic perspective needed for effective leadership. Executives must navigate ambiguity, build relationships based on trust, and make judgment calls that often involve ethical considerations beyond mere numbers.

Healthcare Providers Beyond Medicine

Beyond traditional medical roles, healthcare providers such as **nurses** and **therapists** engage deeply with patients' physical and emotional well-being. These professions demand empathy, patience, and adaptability—traits inherently human.

For example:

- Nurses often serve as primary caregivers who interpret patients' non-verbal cues.

- Physical therapists design personalized rehabilitation programs responding dynamically to patient progress.

Such personalized care requires a level of interpersonal interaction that AI has yet to achieve.

These examples illustrate diverse fields where human qualities remain paramount despite technological advancements in artificial intelligence. Each profession underscores essential attributes—empathy in healthcare providers or creativity in artists—that continue to set humans apart from machines.

High Paying Jobs Resistant to AI Replacement

Healthcare Professionals

Healthcare remains a domain where human qualities are irreplaceable. **Doctors, surgeons, and nurses** not only require extensive knowledge but also the ability to empathize with patients. Complex diagnostic processes, combined with human intuition, create a nuanced approach to patient care that cannot be replicated by algorithms. A surgeon's skillful hands and quick decision-making in the operating room highlight the limitations of robotic precision.

> *Example*: Dr. Atul Gawande, renowned surgeon and writer, underscores that while AI can assist in diagnostics, the intricate understanding of patient history and emotional support provided by human doctors is irreplaceable.

Creative Industries

Artistry and innovation thrive on human creativity. **Writers, musicians, artists**, and even **advertising executives** rely on unique perspectives and emotional depth. AI can generate content based on patterns but lacks the genuine creative spark that drives human expression. The distinctiveness of personal style and the ability to evoke emotions through art form a barrier against automation.

> *Example*: Consider J.K. Rowling's creation of the Harry Potter series. The richness of her characters and imaginative world-building stem from her unique life

experiences—elements an algorithm simply cannot mimic.

Legal Professionals

The legal field requires a blend of critical thinking, empathy, and ethical judgment. While AI can aid in legal research by sifting through vast amounts of data for precedents and statutes, **lawyers**, **judges**, and **mediators** engage in complex argumentation and negotiation processes that demand deep understanding and interpretation of human behavior.

> *Example*: Ruth Bader Ginsburg's career exemplifies how legal decisions often hinge on nuanced interpretations of law interwoven with societal values—an area where machine learning falls short.

Education Sector

Instructors play pivotal roles beyond mere information delivery. **Teachers**, **professors**, and **educational consultants** foster environments conducive to learning through personalized interactions, mentorship, and encouragement. They adapt teaching methods to fit individual student needs—something AI struggles with due to its lack of emotional intelligence.

Example: Professor John Keating from "Dead Poets Society" demonstrates how inspiring students goes beyond textbook knowledge; it involves connecting on an emotional level to ignite passion for learning.

Executive Management

Leadership positions necessitate strategic vision, charisma, and motivational skills that are inherently human traits. CEOs, COOs, and other C-suite executives navigate complex organizational landscapes through interpersonal relationships, ethical considerations, and adaptive strategies in response to market dynamics.

Example: Steve Jobs' innovative leadership at Apple illustrates how visionary thinking combined with charismatic communication can drive an organization to new heights—a feat difficult for AI-driven systems focused purely on data analytics.

Mental Health Professionals

Mental health is another field where human interaction is paramount. **Psychologists, psychiatrists**, and **therapists** provide crucial support through empathy, understanding, and personalized treatment plans based on comprehensive assessments of individual experiences.

Example: Carl Rogers' client-centered therapy emphasizes empathy as central to effective mental health treatment—an element impossible for AI to replicate authentically.

This examination reveals that while AI excels at handling data-intensive tasks, professions requiring emotional intelligence, creativity, complex decision-making processes remain securely within the realm of human capability.

What to Look for in an AI Resistant Career Field

Finding a career that can withstand the rise of artificial intelligence (AI) is like trying to find your way through a world that's constantly changing due to technology. The secret is to know what makes us human—qualities that machines just can't replicate.

1. Complex Problem-Solving and Critical Thinking

Jobs that require deep thinking and solving complex problems are less likely to be taken over by AI. These jobs need:

- **Analytical Skills**: Fields like data science, engineering, and strategic consulting require understanding complex data and making decisions based on it.

- **Decision-Making**: Leaders and policymakers often make important decisions that affect many people, which requires judgment that goes beyond algorithms.

These roles depend on human traits like intuition, experience, and the ability to predict outcomes—things machines struggle with.

2. Emotional Intelligence and Human Interaction

Jobs that focus on emotional intelligence (EI) and face-to-face communication are mostly safe from AI takeover. Some examples are:

- **Healthcare**: Medical professionals like doctors, nurses, and therapists offer not just treatment but also emotional support and personalized care.

- **Counseling**: Psychologists and social workers help people with their mental health by understanding emotions in ways machines can't.

Empathy is at the heart of these jobs, showing how important human connection is in areas where machines fall short.

3. Creativity and Innovation

Jobs that revolve around creativity cannot be replaced by AI because they are unpredictable and original by nature. Think about careers in:

- **The Arts**: Artists, musicians, and writers create works that touch people emotionally.

- **Entrepreneurship**: Innovators who find gaps in the market and come up with new solutions rely heavily on creative thinking.

While machines can imitate patterns, they lack the unique spark of human creativity that leads to groundbreaking ideas.

4. Adaptability and Continuous Learning

Jobs that require flexibility are essential as they change along with technological advancements. These include:

- **Technology Specialists**: IT experts and software developers must always learn new things to keep up with emerging technologies.

- **Educators**: Teachers have to adjust their lessons to include new learning tools while still being personal.

Being adaptable ensures that individuals can change when necessary, welcoming new situations instead of being pushed out by them.

5. Synthesis of Skills

In general, careers resistant to AI often combine different skill sets. Look at roles such as:

- **Product Managers**: They mix technical knowledge with market understanding and team leadership.

- **Clinical Researchers**: They combine scientific rigor with innovative trial designs to push medical boundaries.

These hybrid jobs show how powerful it is to mix analytical skills with creativity and empathy—a combination machines find hard to imitate.

Jobs and Careers That AI Can't Easily Replace

- **Surgeon** - Requires complex decision-making and manual dexterity that AI can't replicate.

- **Psychiatrist** - Involves deep human interaction and understanding of mental health.

- **Anesthesiologist** - Needs precise real-time adjustments and patient monitoring.

- **Dentist** - Combines technical skill and patient care that AI cannot fully automate.

- **Orthodontist** - Requires personalized treatment plans and manual adjustments.

- **Optometrist** - Involves patient interaction and personalized eye care.

- **Pharmacist** - Requires professional judgment and patient counseling.

- **Veterinarian** - Involves hands-on care and diagnosis of animals.

- **Physician Assistant** - Requires patient interaction and clinical decision-making.

- **Nurse Practitioner** - Involves personalized patient care and health management.

- **Physical Therapist** - Requires tailored treatment plans and hands-on therapy.

- **Occupational Therapist** - Involves customized care plans and patient interaction.

- **Speech-Language Pathologist** - Requires personalized therapy and human interaction.

- **Radiation Therapist** - Involves patient-specific treatment and monitoring.

- **Chiropractor** - Requires manual adjustments and personalized care.

- **Clinical Laboratory Technician** - Involves complex analysis and interpretation of lab results.

- **Biomedical Engineer** - Requires innovative problem-solving and design skills.

- **Environmental Engineer** - Involves complex problem-solving and regulatory compliance.

- **Civil Engineer** - Requires creative design and project management.

- **Aerospace Engineer** - Involves innovative design and testing of aerospace systems.

- **Electrical Engineer** - Requires complex problem-solving and design skills.

- **Mechanical Engineer** - Involves creative design and engineering solutions.

- **Chemical Engineer** - Requires innovative process design and safety management.

- **Software Developer** - Involves creative problem-solving and design of software solutions.

- **Data Scientist** - Requires advanced analytical skills and interpretation of data.

- **Cybersecurity Analyst** - Involves dynamic problem-solving and threat management.

- **Information Systems Manager** - Requires strategic planning and management of IT systems.

- **IT Project Manager** - Involves managing complex projects and human resources.

- **Network Architect** - Requires advanced design and optimization of networks.

- **Database Administrator** - Involves complex database management and security.

- **Market Research Analyst** - Requires human insight into market trends and consumer behavior.

- **Financial Analyst** - Involves complex financial analysis and strategic recommendations.

- **Actuary** - Requires advanced mathematical skills and risk assessment.

- **Personal Financial Advisor** - Involves personalized financial planning and advice.

- **Management Consultant** - Requires human insight into organizational improvement.

- **HR Manager** - Involves managing human resources and complex interpersonal issues.

- **Sales Manager** - Requires human interaction and strategic sales planning.

- **Marketing Manager** - Involves creative strategy and market understanding.

- **Operations Manager** - Requires dynamic problem-solving and process optimization.

- **Construction Manager** - Involves project management and on-site decision-making.

- **Project Manager** - Requires coordination of complex projects and human resources.

- **Real Estate Manager** - Involves personalized client interactions and property management.

- **Public Relations Specialist** - Requires strategic communication and human interaction.

- **Lawyer** - Involves complex legal analysis and client advocacy.

- **Judge** - Requires human judgment and interpretation of the law.

- **Legislator** - Involves human insight and decision-making in policymaking.

- **School Principal** - Requires management of educational staff and student interactions.

- **University Professor** - Involves personalized teaching and academic research.

- **Special Education Teacher** - Requires individualized teaching and student care.

- **Therapist/Counselor** - Involves deep human interaction and personalized therapy.

- **Respiratory Therapist** - Requires patient-specific care and manual respiratory treatments.

- **Dietitian/Nutritionist** - Involves personalized dietary planning and counseling.

- **Art Director** - Requires creative vision and artistic skills.

- **Graphic Designer** - Involves creative design and visual communication.

- **Interior Designer** - Requires personalized design solutions and client interaction.

- **Urban Planner** - Involves complex planning and human-centered design.

- **Archaeologist** - Requires human interpretation of artifacts and historical sites.

- **Historian** - Involves research and interpretation of historical events and documents.

- **Psychologist** - Requires deep understanding of human behavior and mental health.

- **Audiologist** - Involves personalized hearing assessments and treatments.

- **Genetic Counselor** - Requires interpreting genetic information and counseling patients.

- **Sociologist** - Involves studying social behavior and human interactions.

- **Anthropologist** - Requires human-centered research and cultural analysis.

- **Museum Curator** - Involves preserving and interpreting artifacts and artworks.

- **Librarian** - Requires managing information and assisting patrons.

- **Event Planner** - Involves coordinating and personalizing events and gatherings.

- **Chef/Head Cook** - Requires culinary creativity and hands-on food preparation.

- **Sommelier** - Involves expert knowledge of wines and personalized recommendations.

- **Barber/Hairdresser** - Requires personalized hair care and styling.

- **Esthetician** - Involves personalized skincare treatments and client interaction.

- **Jeweler** - Requires manual craftsmanship and creative design.

- **Florist** - Involves creative floral design and personalized arrangements.

- **Fashion Designer** - Requires creative vision and manual garment creation.

- **Furniture Maker** - Involves skilled craftsmanship and personalized designs.

- **Landscape Architect** - Requires creative design and environmental planning.

- **Marine Biologist** - Involves field research and complex data analysis.

- **Forestry Manager** - Requires managing natural resources and environmental planning.

- **Zoologist** - Involves studying animal behavior and ecosystems.

- **Wildlife Biologist** - Requires field research and species conservation efforts.

- **Park Ranger** - Involves managing natural parks and human interaction.

- **Agricultural Scientist** - Requires research and innovation in farming practices.

- **Horticulturist** - Involves plant cultivation and personalized landscaping.

- **Meteorologist** - Requires weather prediction and complex data interpretation.

- **Astronomer** - Involves studying celestial objects and interpreting data.

- **Geologist** - Requires field research and interpretation of geological data.

- **Marine Engineer** - Involves designing and maintaining marine equipment and vessels.

- **Ship Captain** - Requires navigation and management of maritime operations.

- **Air Traffic Controller** - Involves real-time decision-making and managing flight operations.

- **Pilot** - Requires manual flying skills and real-time decision-making.

- **Paramedic** - Involves emergency medical care and patient interaction.

- **Firefighter** - Requires physical skills and real-time decision-making.

- **Police Officer** - Involves law enforcement and complex human interactions.

- **Detective/Criminal Investigator** - Requires solving crimes and human intuition.

- **Correctional Officer** - Involves managing inmate populations and maintaining order.

- **Security Specialist** - Requires real-time threat assessment and management.

- **Emergency Management Director** - Involves planning and responding to emergencies.

- **Speechwriter** - Requires personalized writing and creative communication skills.

- **Public Health Administrator** - Involves managing health programs and community interaction.

- **Nonprofit Manager** - Requires managing nonprofit organizations and human resources.

- **Clergy/Pastor** - Involves spiritual guidance and deep human interaction.

Transitioning to AI-Resistant Jobs

What Are Transferable Skills?

Transferable skills are abilities that can be used in different jobs and industries. Unlike specific skills that are limited to certain tasks or technologies, transferable skills are broader and can be applied in various situations. These skills include:

- **Critical Thinking**: The ability to analyze information and make decisions based on evidence.

- **Communication**: The ability to convey ideas clearly and effectively, both verbally and in writing.

- **Adaptability**: The ability to adjust to new environments and changes quickly.

- **Problem-Solving**: The ability to identify challenges and come up with effective solutions.

These skills are essential for career resilience, helping professionals navigate changes in the job market.

Why Are Transferable Skills Important?

In today's world, where artificial intelligence (AI) and automation are becoming more prevalent, having transferable skills is crucial. Being able to adapt and change is not just an advantage but necessary for survival in this evolving landscape. Companies are looking for individuals who can fit into different roles and bring a diverse set of skills that promote innovation and efficiency.

Studies show that jobs requiring high levels of social interaction and emotional intelligence are less likely to be automated. For example, roles in healthcare, education, and creative industries still prioritize human skills over technical abilities. This trend highlights the importance of transferable skills in maintaining employability.

Examples of Transferable Skills

Here are some examples of transferable skills that can be valuable in AI-resistant jobs:

1. **Critical Thinking**: The ability to analyze situations, identify problems, and come up with effective solutions.

2. **Communication**: Being able to communicate clearly and effectively with others.

3. **Adaptability**: Being open to change and able to adjust quickly.

4. **Emotional Intelligence (EQ)**: Understanding your own

emotions and those of others.

5. **Problem-Solving**: Finding solutions to challenges or obstacles.

6. **Teamwork**: Working well with others towards a common goal.

7. **Leadership**: Inspiring and guiding others towards achieving objectives.

8. **Time Management**: Prioritizing tasks effectively to maximize productivity.

Real-World Examples

Here are some real-world examples of how transferable skills can be applied:

- A software engineer transitioning into a project management role within the tech industry:

- Uses critical thinking to analyze user requirements effectively.

- Communicates project goals clearly to stakeholders.

- Adapts quickly by learning new project management software.

- A teacher moving into corporate training:

- Applies emotional intelligence by understanding trainee needs.

- Uses problem-solving skills to develop engaging training modules.

- Demonstrates leadership by motivating employees towards continuous learning.

These examples show how transferable skills can help professionals move between different careers while also being resilient against AI disruptions.

Understanding what transferable skills are allows professionals like you recognize their inherent value beyond traditional job boundaries. This recognition paves the way for strategic career planning aimed at thriving amidst technological advancements rather than being overshadowed by them—making adaptability and resilience not just qualities but necessities for future success.

Building a Personalized Learning Plan

Creating a personalized learning plan is like making a roadmap for your career. It makes sure that the skills you learn match up with your job goals and the changing job market. By following certain steps and using resources wisely, you can create a plan that helps you succeed in jobs less likely to be affected by AI.

Steps to Create a Learning Plan

1. **Self-Assessment**: Start by looking at your current skills, strengths, and weaknesses. This self-reflection helps you find areas where you need improvement to stay competitive.

2. **Set Clear Goals**: Define what you want to achieve in both

the short-term and long-term. Whether it's mastering new software, getting certified, or developing soft skills, clear goals give you direction.

3. **Identify Required Skills**: Research the skills that are in demand for your desired career path. Sources like job descriptions, industry reports, and professional forums can provide insights into what employers want.

4. **Create a Timeline**: Set realistic deadlines for reaching each goal. A timeline keeps you accountable and breaks down the learning process into smaller parts.

5. **Select Learning Resources**: Choose suitable materials and platforms to support your learning. Depending on how you learn best, options like books, online courses, workshops, or mentorship programs can be beneficial.

6. **Monitor Progress**: Regularly check your progress against the established goals. Make adjustments to the plan as necessary to stay on course or accommodate any changes in career objectives.

Aligning Personal Goals with Job Market Demands

Aligning personal goals with market demands is crucial for staying relevant in an ever-changing job landscape.

Conduct Market Research

Conduct thorough research on current trends and future predictions within your industry. Use this data to tailor your learning plan to include emerging skills that are gaining traction.

Perform Gap Analysis

Compare your existing skill set with those required by trending job roles. This analysis will highlight areas where additional training or education is necessary.

Maintain Flexibility

Remain adaptable in your approach. The job market evolves rapidly, requiring continual reassessment of priorities and goals.

Example: An aspiring data analyst might discover through market research that proficiency in Python is increasingly sought after over traditional Excel skills. Adjusting their learning plan to include Python programming courses would be an astute alignment of personal goals with market needs.

Utilizing Resources Effectively

Effective resource utilization maximizes the impact of your personalized learning plan.

Explore Online Courses

Platforms like Coursera, Udemy, and edX offer courses ranging from technical skills to leadership development. These courses often include certifications that can enhance your resume.

Read Books and Publications

Reading industry-specific books and journals keeps you updated on theoretical knowledge and practical applications.

Attend Workshops and Seminars

Attending events allows for hands-on experience and networking opportunities with professionals who share similar interests.

Join Mentorship Programs

Engaging with mentors provides personalized advice, feedback, and support tailored to your career path.

Quote: "Learning is not attained by chance; it must be sought for with ardor and attended to with diligence." – Abigail Adams

To illustrate effective resource utilization:

Case Study: Jane, an IT professional looking to transition into cybersecurity, enrolled in multiple online courses specific to cybersecurity techniques while simultaneously participating in local cybersecurity workshops. She also connected with industry mentors through LinkedIn who guided her career shift successfully.

Importance of Critical Thinking and Problem Solving

Role of Critical Thinking in AI-Resistant Jobs

In the ever-changing job market, **critical thinking** has become more important than ever. As artificial intelligence takes over repetitive tasks, jobs that require advanced thinking skills are safe from automation. Critical thinking is the ability to analyze information and make judgments, something machines still struggle to do in complicated human situations.

AI-resistant jobs often require quick decisions based on limited information. For instance, healthcare workers must diagnose and treat patients using a mix of medical knowledge and personal interaction—tasks that demand deep critical thinking. Similarly, financial analysts need to understand market trends and predict future movements, which requires strong analytical skills.

Techniques for Enhancing Problem-Solving Abilities

Improving your problem-solving skills is like sharpening a tool; it needs regular practice and different methods:

1. **Root Cause Analysis (RCA):** Find out the main cause of a problem instead of just fixing the symptoms. This ensures long-lasting solutions.

2. **Mind Mapping:** Use diagrams to visualize problems and solutions. This helps break down complex issues into smaller parts.

3. **Scenario Planning:** Think about different future scenarios and plan how to respond. This is especially useful in strategic roles where foresight is important.

4. **The 5 Whys Technique:** Keep asking "why" multiple times to dig deeper into the core cause of the problem.

Using these techniques encourages a mindset focused on creative solutions, making individuals invaluable in their positions.

Real-life Examples from Industry Leaders

Industry leaders demonstrate how critical thinking and problem-solving can lead to success:

- **Elon Musk at SpaceX**: When faced with multiple failures during rocket launches, Musk used thorough analysis and repeated testing to find and fix problems, eventually achieving remarkable advancements in space travel.

- **Indra Nooyi at PepsiCo**: Confronting declining soda sales, Nooyi led a transformation by diversifying the company's product line towards healthier options. Her strategic foresight and analytical skills not only reversed declining trends but also positioned PepsiCo as a leader in the health-conscious market segment.

Both examples show how critical thinking can help organizations overcome challenges and set them up for long-term success.

Enhancing Analytical Skills

Analytical skills are fundamental to critical thinking:

- **Data Interpretation**: Get better at understanding data by taking courses on statistics or data science.

- **Pattern Recognition**: Engage in activities like puzzles or coding that improve your ability to spot patterns.

- **Continuous Learning**: Stay updated with industry trends by reading relevant literature or attending seminars.

These strategies ensure that your analytical abilities remain sharp, enabling you to tackle complex problems efficiently.

Understanding the importance of critical thinking and problem-solving highlights their irreplaceable value in AI-resistant jobs. These cognitive abilities not only set humans apart from machines but also drive innovation and strategic progress within industries.

Developing Emotional Intelligence and Empathy

Why Emotional Intelligence Matters in the Workplace

In jobs that can't be easily replaced by AI, emotional intelligence (EI) is key to long-term success. Daniel Goleman, a top expert on EI, defines it as the ability to recognize, understand, and manage our own emotions while also recognizing, understanding, and influencing the emotions of others. This skill set is invaluable in any professional setting where human interaction plays a pivotal role.

Why is emotional intelligence so critical?

- **Better Communication:** People with high EI can handle complex social situations easily, making them great communicators. They can pick up on body language and respond well to their coworkers' needs.

- **Resolving Conflicts:** Emotionally intelligent employees are skilled at settling disputes by understanding different viewpoints and finding common ground.

- **Leadership Skills:** Leaders with strong EI create an atmosphere of trust and respect, which can boost team performance and morale.

How to Develop Empathy

Empathy, often seen as a part of emotional intelligence, is crucial for building strong relationships. It helps people understand and share someone else's feelings, forming the basis for good teamwork.

How can you develop empathy?

1. **Active Listening:**

- Be fully present in conversations without interrupting.

- Repeat back what you hear to show you understand.

1. **Seeing from Another's Perspective:**

- Try to imagine yourself in someone else's situation.

- Think about how you would feel if you were in their shoes.

1. **Mindfulness Techniques:**

- Mindfulness meditation can boost self-awareness and empathy.

- Practices like deep breathing or guided imagery help focus on other people's experiences.

1. **Reading Fiction:**

- Books introduce readers to different viewpoints and life experiences.

- Research shows that reading fiction increases empathy by letting people experience life through characters.

How It Affects Team Dynamics and Leadership

Emotional intelligence and empathy don't just impact individual interactions; they also shape how teams work together and how effective leaders are. Teams led by emotionally intelligent leaders show higher levels of trust, cooperation, and resilience.

Key effects include:

- **Better Teamwork:** Teams with high EI work better together because members know each other's strengths and weaknesses.

- **More Innovation:** A leader who promotes an emotionally intelligent culture encourages taking risks and creative problem-solving.

- **Higher Employee Retention:** Workers are more likely to stay with companies where they feel understood, appreciated, and emotionally supported.

Example: Satya Nadella – Microsoft

Satya Nadella's time as CEO of Microsoft shows the impact of emotional intelligence in leadership. When he became CEO in 2014, Nadella made empathy a core value. His strategy changed Microsoft's culture from one marked by internal competition to one centered on collaboration and innovation. As a result:

- Microsoft saw significant growth in employee satisfaction

scores.

- The company experienced a rise in market value, reflecting its renewed energy under empathetic leadership.

Quote from Satya Nadella:

"The one attribute that I think is most useful when you're trying to lead change is not even IQ; it's EQ."

By focusing on emotional intelligence and empathy, professionals can not only protect their jobs from automation but also improve their leadership skills in increasingly people-focused workplaces.

Acquiring Advanced Technical Skills

Understanding the landscape of **AI-resistant jobs** requires an appreciation for advanced technical skills. In a world increasingly dominated by automation and artificial intelligence, certain technical proficiencies remain indispensable. These skills not only serve as a bulwark against obsolescence but also provide a competitive edge in the job market.

In-Demand Technical Skills for AI-Resistant Roles

Several technical skills stand out for their enduring relevance:
- **Data Science**: The ability to analyze and interpret complex data sets is invaluable. Data scientists are crucial in making informed decisions based on data insights, a task that machines can assist with but not entirely replace.

- **Cybersecurity**: Protecting digital infrastructure from cyber threats is an arena where human expertise remains paramount. Cybersecurity experts develop strategies to safeguard sensitive information, ensuring the integrity of organizational operations.

- **Software Development**: Crafting and maintaining software solutions require creativity and problem-solving abilities that AI cannot fully replicate. Developers continuously adapt to new languages and frameworks, keeping this role highly dynamic.

Resources for Acquiring Technical Knowledge

The journey to mastering these skills is facilitated by numerous resources:

- **Online Courses**: Platforms like Coursera, Udemy, and edX offer specialized courses in data science, cybersecurity, and software development. These courses are designed by industry experts and often include practical projects.

- **Bootcamps**: Intensive bootcamps such as General Assembly or Flatiron School focus on immersive learning experiences. They provide hands-on training in coding, data analysis, and other technical fields within a short time frame.

- **Certifications**: Recognized certifications add credibility to one's skill set. For instance:

- *Certified Information Systems Security Professional (CISSP)* for cybersecurity

- *Microsoft Certified: Azure Data Scientist Associate* for data science

- *Certified Software Development Professional (CSDP)* for software development

Case Studies of Successful Transitions

Real-life examples underscore the effectiveness of acquiring advanced technical skills:

Data Science Transformation

Jane Doe transitioned from a marketing analyst to a data scientist after completing an online course on Coursera and earning her certification from Microsoft. Her newfound expertise allowed her to leverage big data analytics in developing targeted marketing strategies, significantly increasing her company's customer engagement rates.

Cybersecurity Expertise

John Smith shifted his career from network administration to cybersecurity by enrolling in a bootcamp at Flatiron School. After obtaining his CISSP certification, he landed a role as a cybersecurity analyst at a major financial institution, where he now leads efforts to fortify the company's defenses against cyber threats.

Software Development Evolution

Emily Johnson moved from graphic design to software development through a combination of self-study on Udemy and participating in coding bootcamps at General Assembly. She now works as a front-end developer for a tech startup, contributing to innovative web applications that enhance user experience.

Metaphorical Insight

Consider these advanced technical skills as tools in an artisan's workshop—each tool serves a unique purpose but collectively they enable the creation of masterpieces that withstand the test of time. Just as artisans refine their craft through practice and learning, professionals must continuously update their technical competencies to stay relevant in an evolving job market.

Investing in advanced technical skills equips individuals with the resilience needed to navigate the complexities of AI-resistant roles. By leveraging available resources and drawing inspiration from successful transitions, one can build a robust foundation for a future-proof career.

Pursuing Relevant Degrees and Certifications

Overview of Educational Pathways

The journey toward an AI-resistant career often begins with the right educational foundation. Relevant degrees play a crucial role in equipping individuals with the knowledge and skills required to thrive in a rapidly evolving job market. Degrees in fields such as:

- **Data Science**

- **Cybersecurity**

- **Human-Computer Interaction**

- **Ethics in Technology**

These programs not only provide technical expertise but also foster critical thinking and problem-solving abilities essential for navigating complex work environments.

Value of Certifications in Technology Fields

While degrees offer broad and comprehensive education, certifications serve as targeted validations of specific skills. They signal to employers that an individual possesses the requisite expertise to excel in particular areas. Certifications can bridge gaps between academic learning and practical application, making them indispensable in professional development.

Key Benefits of Certifications:

- **Immediate Relevance:** Certifications often focus on current technologies and methodologies, ensuring relevance to present industry standards.

- **Specialized Knowledge:** They allow professionals to hone in on niche areas, becoming experts in specific domains.

- **Career Advancement:** Holding a certification can make candidates more competitive for promotions or new job opportunities, leading to higher earning potential.

Examples of Respected Certifications

Numerous certifications have gained recognition for their rigorous standards and industry relevance. Here are a few worth considering:

- **Certified Information Systems Security Professional (CISSP):**Recognized globally, CISSP is ideal for those looking to advance in cybersecurity. It covers essential topics like risk management, network security, and cryptography.

- **Project Management Professional (PMP):**This certification is valuable for those aiming to lead projects effectively. It emphasizes project planning, execution, monitoring, and closing.

- **Google Professional Data Engineer:**Focused on data engineering, this certification validates skills in designing data processing systems, ensuring data security, and optimizing performance.

- **Certified Ethical Hacker (CEH):**For those interested in cybersecurity from an offensive standpoint, CEH certifies your ability to think like a hacker to better protect systems.

- **AWS Certified Solutions Architect:**This certification is crucial for professionals working with Amazon Web Services (AWS), demonstrating their ability to design scalable cloud architectures.

Strategic Integration of Degrees and Certifications

Combining degrees with certifications can create a robust professional profile that stands out in the competitive job market. For example:

- A degree in Data Science paired with a Google Professional

Data Engineer certification offers both theoretical understanding and practical implementation skills.

- A background in Computer Science complemented by PMP
certification equips professionals with technical knowledge
and project management capabilities.

By strategically integrating both educational pathways and certifications, one not only gains comprehensive knowledge but also
demonstrates commitment to continuous learning—a trait highly
valued by employers.

Real-World Applications

Consider the case of Jane Doe, who transitioned from a traditional IT
role to a cybersecurity expert. With a degree in Information Technology and CISSP certification under her belt, she successfully navigated
the complexities of her new role. Her story exemplifies how degrees
provide foundational knowledge while certifications offer specialized
skills critical for career advancement.

In another instance, John Smith pursued an MBA alongside his
PMP certification. This combination enabled him to climb the corporate ladder swiftly by leveraging his management acumen along
with his project management expertise.

The synergy between degrees and certifications cannot be overstated; it prepares professionals not just for existing roles but also equips
them for future challenges posed by technological advancements.

Degrees and certifications form the cornerstone of professional
development in AI-resistant careers—one providing depth of knowledge, the other offering breadth through specialized skill sets.

Gaining Experience through Internships and Volunteering

Importance of Hands-On Experience in Career Transition

Gaining practical experience is a cornerstone in transitioning to AI-resistant jobs. Hands-on experience provides real-world insights that theoretical knowledge simply cannot. It bridges the gap between classroom learning and actual workplace demands, making candidates more adaptable and competent. This immersive exposure to industry practices enables professionals to navigate complex problems, refine their skills, and understand the nuances of their chosen field.

Internships offer structured environments where individuals can apply their academic learning to real-world scenarios. For instance, a software engineering internship might involve coding projects that directly contribute to a company's product line, offering invaluable experience that textbooks alone cannot provide.

Volunteering serves as another potent avenue for gaining hands-on experience. Non-profit organizations often need skilled volunteers to manage projects, run community programs, or develop strategic plans. Such opportunities enable individuals to hone their skills while contributing to meaningful causes.

How to Find Opportunities in Your Field of Interest

Identifying suitable internships and volunteering roles requires a proactive approach:

1. **Research**: Start by identifying companies and organizations aligned with your career goals. Websites like LinkedIn, Glassdoor, and Indeed regularly list internship opportunities.

2. **Network**: Utilize professional networks to uncover hidden opportunities. Attending industry conferences, webinars, and local meetups can connect you with potential employers.

3. **University Career Services**: Most educational institutions have career services departments that offer internship placement assistance.

4. **Online Platforms**: Websites such as InternMatch, Idealist, and Handshake specialize in listing internships and volunteer positions across various fields.

5. **Direct Outreach**: Don't hesitate to directly contact organizations expressing your interest in potential internship or volunteer roles.

Networking Benefits through Volunteering

Volunteering offers more than just skill development; it opens doors to extensive networking opportunities:

- **Professional Connections**: Working alongside seasoned professionals allows you to build relationships that can lead to job referrals or mentorship opportunities.

- **Visibility**: Volunteering showcases your commitment and work ethic, making you a memorable candidate when job openings arise.

- **Skill Demonstration**: Volunteering provides a platform for demonstrating your abilities in live projects, often leading to unsolicited job offers from impressed stakeholders.

Consider the story of Jane Smith, who volunteered at a local tech startup while completing her computer science degree. Her exceptional performance caught the eye of the company's CEO, who later offered her a full-time position upon graduation.

Leveraging Internships for Career Growth

Internships can serve as stepping stones toward long-term career goals:
- **Skill Refinement**: Internships allow for the application of theoretical knowledge in practical settings, enabling skill refinement under professional supervision.

- **Resume Building**: Real-world experience enhances your resume, making you more appealing to future employers.

- **Potential Employment**: Many companies use internships as a pipeline for recruiting full-time employees.

A case in point is John Doe's journey from an intern at Google to securing a permanent role as a data analyst due to his outstanding performance during his internship tenure.

Networking and Professional Associations

Strategies for Effective Networking in the Digital Age

Networking has evolved significantly with the advent of digital platforms. In today's interconnected world, developing a robust network is about more than just attending events or exchanging business cards. Effective networking strategies include:

- **Leveraging Social Media Platforms**: LinkedIn, Twitter, and even niche platforms like GitHub for developers are essential tools. These platforms facilitate connections with industry leaders and peers globally.

- **Participating in Online Communities**: Engaging in forums, discussion groups, and virtual meetups can establish your presence and expertise in your field.

- **Maintaining Consistent Communication**: Regularly updating your network on your professional milestones and insights through posts or newsletters keeps you top-of-mind.

- **Utilizing Video Conferencing Tools**: Virtual coffee chats or informational interviews via Zoom or Skype can break geographical barriers and foster deeper connections.

Digital networking not only broadens your reach but also allows for more targeted interactions. According to a study by *Harvard Business Review*, professionals who actively engage online are 60% more likely to achieve career growth.

Benefits of Joining Professional Associations

Professional associations offer a myriad of advantages that extend well beyond networking opportunities. These benefits include:

- **Access to Exclusive Resources**: Members gain access to specialized publications, research reports, and industry data that aren't available to the general public.

- **Professional Development Opportunities**: Many associations provide workshops, webinars, and certifications tailored to industry-specific skills.

- **Advocacy and Representation**: Associations often lobby on behalf of their members' interests at the governmental level, advocating for policies that can enhance career prospects.

- **Recognition and Credibility**: Being a member of a reputable association adds a layer of credibility to your professional profile.

Consider the *American Marketing Association (AMA)* as an example. Membership offers access to cutting-edge marketing resources, certification programs, and an extensive network of marketing professionals. This connection can be instrumental in staying updated on industry trends and best practices.

Success Stories from Industry Connections

Real-world examples underscore the transformative impact of strategic networking and active involvement in professional associations:

1. Sarah's Journey in Cybersecurity

- Sarah began her career as an IT specialist with limited connections in cybersecurity. She joined the *Information Systems Security Association (ISSA)* where she participated in local chapter meetings and volunteered at events. Her active involvement led to mentorship opportunities and eventually a senior role at a leading cybersecurity firm.

1. **John's Ascent in Project Management**

- John was a mid-level project manager looking to advance his career. He became an active member of the *Project Management Institute (PMI)*, attending annual conferences and contributing articles to their journal. By leveraging these networking opportunities, John was able to secure a position as Director of Project Management at a Fortune 500 company.

1. **Emma's Breakthrough in Data Science**

- Emma transitioned from academia into data science by joining the *Data Science Society*. Through participation in hackathons and online communities facilitated by the society, she connected with key industry figures who provided guidance on her projects. This network ultimately helped her land her dream job at a major tech firm.

The power of networking lies not just in expanding one's contact list but in building meaningful relationships that foster mutual growth. Professional associations play an integral role in providing structured environments where these relationships can flourish.

Networking and professional associations form the backbone of career growth strategies in today's dynamic job market.

Staying Updated with Industry Trends

Importance of Staying Informed About Technological Advancements

In an era dominated by rapid technological advancements, keeping abreast of industry trends is non-negotiable. The labor market is in a state of constant flux, driven by innovations that can render certain skills obsolete while making others indispensable. **Continuous learning** is the key to staying relevant and competitive.

Consider the advent of artificial intelligence and machine learning technologies. These advancements have revolutionized industries from healthcare to finance, creating new roles such as AI ethics consultants and data scientists. Ignoring these shifts can leave professionals unprepared and outpaced.

> "The illiterate of the 21st century will not be those who cannot read and write, but those who cannot learn, unlearn, and relearn." – Alvin Toffler

Resources for Tracking Industry Changes

To navigate the complexities of evolving industry landscapes, leveraging a variety of resources is essential:
- **Blogs**: Regularly reading industry-specific blogs can provide insights into emerging trends and best practices. Websites like *TechCrunch*, *Wired*, and *Harvard Business Review* offer

valuable analysis on technological advancements.

- **Podcasts**: For those who prefer auditory learning, podcasts such as *a16z* by Andreessen Horowitz or *The AI Alignment Podcast* offer deep dives into current tech developments.

- **Webinars and Online Courses**: Platforms like Coursera, Udemy, and LinkedIn Learning frequently update their content to reflect the latest industry standards.

- **Research Papers and Journals**: Academic journals often contain pioneering research that can signal future industry directions. Websites like Google Scholar make finding relevant papers straightforward.

These resources serve as a foundation for understanding how new technologies impact your field, allowing you to adapt your strategies accordingly.

Adapting Career Strategies Based on Trends

Adapting to labor market changes requires a proactive approach. Professionals must analyze trends critically to identify which skills will be in demand. Here are some steps to consider:

1. **Skill Mapping**: Evaluate your current skill set against emerging trends. Identify gaps that need addressing.

2. **Upskilling**: Enroll in courses or training programs that focus on high-demand areas such as cybersecurity, data analytics, and cloud computing.

3. **Networking**: Engage with industry leaders through con-

ferences, webinars, and social media platforms like LinkedIn
to gain insights from those at the forefront of technological
change.

4. **Experimentation**: Don't hesitate to experiment with new
tools or methodologies within your current role. Being an
early adopter can position you as an innovator.

A real-life example comes from Satya Nadella's transformation of
Microsoft. Understanding the shift towards cloud computing and
AI, Nadella pivoted Microsoft's strategy towards these areas. This not
only revitalized the company but also positioned it as a leader in cloud
services.

Adapting career strategies isn't just about reacting to changes; it's
about anticipating them. This foresight can lead to career resilience in
an unpredictable job market.

Staying updated with industry trends is akin to navigating a ship
through ever-changing waters; it requires vigilance, adaptability, and
a willingness to chart new courses based on emerging data points.

Emphasizing Creativity and Innovation

Creativity is a key factor in jobs that are resistant to AI, providing
protection against the rise of automation. While machines are great
at doing repetitive tasks accurately, they struggle when it comes to the
complex demands of creative thinking. Humans have an unmatched
ability to come up with new ideas, connect different concepts, and
imagine unique solutions that artificial intelligence cannot replicate.

Role of Creativity in AI-Resistant Jobs

The importance of creativity in today's job market cannot be emphasized enough. Many industries, such as marketing and product development, heavily rely on innovative thinking to stay competitive.

1. Marketing and Advertising

Creating compelling campaigns requires an understanding of human emotions and cultural nuances that algorithms cannot grasp.

2. Product Development

Imagining future needs and designing products that resonate with users requires a combination of creativity and practical knowledge.

3. Consulting

Providing tailored solutions to individual client challenges necessitates creative problem-solving skills.

Techniques to Foster Innovative Thinking

Creating an environment that encourages innovation involves intentional strategies aimed at enhancing creative abilities.

1. Diverse Teams

Bringing together individuals from different backgrounds creates a melting pot of ideas. This diversity sparks creativity by combining various perspectives.

2. Brainstorming Sessions

Organized brainstorming sessions promote free-flowing ideas without immediate criticism, allowing even the most unconventional thoughts to emerge.

3. Continuous Learning

Exploring new fields and subjects broadens one's cognitive horizons and fuels innovative thinking.

Practical Exercises for Creative Thinking

- **Mind Mapping:** Visualizing connections between different ideas can lead to unexpected insights.

- **SCAMPER Technique:** This involves asking questions about existing processes or products to identify potential areas for innovation (Substitute, Combine, Adapt, Modify, Put to another use, Eliminate, Reverse).

- **Role-Playing:** Stepping into different characters or scenarios can provide fresh angles on a problem.

Examples from Innovative Companies

Several industry leaders demonstrate how nurturing creativity leads to groundbreaking achievements.

- **Google's 20% Time Policy:** Employees are encouraged to spend 20% of their time working on projects they are passionate about. This policy has given birth to successful innovations like Gmail and Google News.

- **Apple's Design Thinking Approach:** Apple's focus on design thinking—an iterative process involving empathy, ideation, prototyping, and testing—has resulted in iconic products such as the iPhone and iPad.

- **Pixar's Braintrust Meetings:** Regular feedback sessions where directors present their work-in-progress to peers ensure that creative ideas are constantly refined and improved.

Balancing Structure with Freedom

Innovation thrives in environments where structure is balanced with freedom. Too much rigidity stifles creativity; too much freedom leads to chaos.

Structured Flexibility:

- Establish clear goals but allow flexibility in how those goals are achieved.

- Encourage experimentation while maintaining accountability.

Creating a Culture of Innovation

Leadership plays a crucial role in fostering a culture where creativity can thrive.

1. **Encourage Risk-Taking:** Leaders should reward innovative efforts even if they fail.

2. **Provide Resources:** Allocating time and financial resources for creative projects signals their importance.

3. **Recognize Achievements:** Celebrating creative successes motivates teams to continue pushing boundaries.

"Creativity is intelligence having fun." – Albert Einstein

Jobs that resist AI require not only technical skills but also the ability to constantly innovate. As organizations strive to stay ahead in an ever-changing landscape, nurturing creativity becomes essential for long-term success.

Attending Workshops and Conferences

Value of Attending Industry Events for Networking and Learning

Engaging in **workshops** and **conferences** is like stepping into a lively marketplace of ideas, buzzing with innovation and opportunity. These professional events are perfect for networking, learning, and personal growth.

Benefits of Attending Industry Events

- **Networking:** It's important to build connections with other professionals in your field. For example, meeting industry leaders can lead to mentorship opportunities that you might not have access to otherwise.

- **Learning:** Workshops often feature the latest content presented by experts in the industry. They discuss real-world applications of theories, providing insights that textbooks or online courses may not cover.

- **Inspiration:** Being exposed to different viewpoints stimulates creativity and can ignite innovative solutions to difficult problems.

How to Choose Relevant Workshops

Choosing the right workshops requires a strategic approach tailored to your career goals. Here's how to navigate this process:

1. **Identify Your Objectives:** Determine what you want to achieve—whether it's acquiring new skills, networking, or gaining industry knowledge.

2. **Research Speakers:** Look up the presenters to ensure they bring value through their expertise and experience.

3. **Review Agendas:** Go through the event schedule for topics that align with your interests and career aspirations.

4. **Seek Recommendations:** Use your professional network for suggestions on must-attend workshops.

By following these steps, you'll get the most out of attending these events.

Personal Anecdotes from Notable Figures Attending Conferences

To show how impactful attending workshops and conferences can be, here are some stories from well-known figures in the industry:

- **Sheryl Sandberg**, COO of Facebook, shares her life-changing experience at the *World Economic Forum*. Participating in high-level discussions not only deepened her understanding but also greatly expanded her network.

- **Elon Musk** has frequently talked about his involvement in tech conferences like *South by Southwest (SXSW)*. These events have played a crucial role in shaping his vision for companies such as SpaceX and Tesla.

- **Satya Nadella**, CEO of Microsoft, credits much of his leadership philosophy to insights gained at different industry gatherings. His attendance at events focused on AI ethics has influenced Microsoft's approach towards responsible AI implementation.

Workshops and conferences provide excellent opportunities for networking, learning, and inspiration. By carefully choosing events that align with personal career goals, professionals can greatly improve their skillset and broaden their professional network. The experiences shared by notable figures highlight the transformative potential these events possess.

Online Courses and E-Learning Platforms

Overview of Popular Online Learning Platforms

The digital age has brought a revolution in education, notably through online courses and e-learning platforms. These platforms offer a *flexible education* model that caters to diverse learning needs and schedules. Here are some of the most popular e-learning platforms:

- **Coursera**: Known for its partnerships with top universities like Stanford and Yale, Coursera provides a vast array of courses on subjects ranging from data science to humanities.

- **Udemy**: With over 155,000 courses, Udemy offers practical skills in areas such as coding, graphic design, and business management.

- **edX**: Founded by Harvard University and MIT, edX offers high-quality courses from leading institutions worldwide.

- **LinkedIn Learning**: Formerly known as Lynda.com, this platform focuses on professional development with courses in leadership, technology, and creative skills.

- **Khan Academy**: Although primarily aimed at school-level education, Khan Academy's resources are invaluable for foundational knowledge in mathematics and science.

Benefits of Online Courses for Skill Development

The advantages of online courses extend beyond mere convenience. They play a crucial role in career transitions toward AI-resistant jobs. Key benefits include:

- **Flexibility**: Learners can access course materials anytime, anywhere, making it easier to balance work, study, and personal commitments.

- **Cost-effectiveness**: Many online courses are more affordable than traditional education programs. Some platforms even offer free courses or financial aid options.

- **Wide Range of Subjects**: The diversity of topics available ensures that learners can find courses tailored to their specific interests and career goals.

- **Self-Paced Learning**: Online courses often allow learners to progress at their own pace, which is particularly beneficial for mastering complex subjects.

- **Skill Validation**: Many e-learning platforms provide certificates upon course completion. These certifications can enhance a resume and validate skills to potential employers.

Recommendations Based on Subject Matter Expertise

Choosing the right course or platform depends on individual goals and the specific skills required for AI-resistant roles. Below are some recommendations based on different areas of expertise:

Data Science and Artificial Intelligence

For those aiming to delve into data science or AI:

- **Coursera's "Machine Learning" by Stanford University**: This course covers fundamental algorithms and practical implementations.

- **Udacity's "Data Scientist Nanodegree"**: A comprehensive program focusing on real-world projects.

Business Management and Leadership

Aspiring leaders can benefit from:

- **Harvard Business School Online's "CORe" Program**: Offers essential business skills in economics, accounting, and analytics.

- **LinkedIn Learning's "Developing Executive Presence"**: Focuses on leadership qualities needed for executive roles.

Creative Fields

For individuals targeting creative industries:

- **Skillshare's "Graphic Design Basics"**: Provides foundational skills in graphic design using software like Adobe Illustrator.

- **Domestika's "Introduction to Photography"**: Covers basic photography techniques from composition to editing.

Real-Life Application Examples

Consider Jane Doe, who transitioned from a marketing role to a data analyst position. She utilized Coursera's "Excel Skills for Business" course combined with edX's "Data Analysis for Life Sciences." Over six months of dedicated learning during weekends and evenings enabled her successful transition. Her journey exemplifies how e-learning platforms provide the tools necessary for career shifts without disrupting daily life.

Similarly, John Smith leveraged LinkedIn Learning's project management courses while working full-time. Within a year, he attained his PMP certification and moved into a managerial position at his company. His story underscores the significance of flexible education models offered by online learning platforms.

E-learning platforms represent an indispensable resource for those seeking to adapt their skillsets in an ever-evolving job market. The flexibility they offer ensures that continuous learning becomes an integral part of professional development strategies.

Developing Leadership and Management Skills

Importance of Leadership Capabilities in AI-Resistant Roles

Leadership skills are essential in the changing job market, especially in roles that are less likely to be automated by AI. Unlike repetitive tasks that machines can do efficiently, leadership requires a combination of strategic thinking, emotional intelligence, and flexible problem-solving skills. These abilities are crucial for driving growth and innovation within organizations.

AI-resistant roles often require:

- **Visionary Thinking**: Leaders must envision the future, set long-term goals, and inspire their teams to achieve them.

- **Strategic Decision-Making**: Making informed decisions that consider short-term impacts and long-term consequences.

- **People Management**: Effective leaders manage diverse teams by leveraging individual strengths and fostering a collaborative environment.

Training Resources Available for Aspiring Leaders

There are many resources available to help develop leadership skills. From formal education to self-directed learning, aspiring leaders have various options to enhance their abilities:

1. **Executive Education Programs**: Institutions like Harvard Business School offer specialized courses focusing on leadership development.

2. **Online Platforms**: Websites such as Coursera and LinkedIn Learning provide extensive courses on management training.

3. **Workshops and Seminars**: Attending industry-specific workshops can provide practical insights into leadership challenges and solutions.

4. **Books and Publications**: Literature from renowned authors like John C. Maxwell or Simon Sinek can offer valuable perspectives on effective leadership.

Real-World Applications of Management Theories

Management theories provide a framework for understanding how organizations work and improving efficiency. Applying these theories in real-life situations can lead to significant improvements in leadership effectiveness:

- **Transformational Leadership**: Encourages leaders to inspire and motivate employees by creating a vision for the future, fostering an environment of intellectual stimulation, and providing individualized consideration.

  Example: Steve Jobs' approach at Apple exemplified transformational leadership by continuously pushing the boundaries of innovation.

- **Situational Leadership**: Suggests that leaders should adjust their style based on the maturity of their team members. This adaptability ensures that the appropriate level of guidance is provided depending on the situation.

  Example: A project manager might adopt a more directive style during a project's initiation phase but shift to a delegative approach as team members become more competent.

- **Servant Leadership**: Focuses on serving the team first, prioritizing their growth, well-being, and overall development over personal gains or traditional power structures.

Example: Companies like Zappos have successfully implemented servant leadership principles to foster a culture of employee empowerment and customer satisfaction.

Techniques for Enhancing Leadership Skills

Becoming an effective leader involves continuous improvement through various methods:

- **Mentorship Programs**: Engaging with experienced mentors can provide valuable guidance and feedback.

- **Self-Assessment Tools**: Instruments like 360-degree feedback help identify strengths and areas for improvement.

- **Real-world Experience**: Taking on challenging projects or interim leadership roles can accelerate skill development.

Industry Perspectives

Organizations across different sectors emphasize the importance of robust leadership:

- In tech companies like Google, leaders encourage a culture of experimentation where failure is seen as a learning opportunity.

- In healthcare, leaders play critical roles in patient care coordination, ensuring both clinical outcomes and patient satisfaction are maximized.

Developing strong leadership skills is not just about climbing the corporate ladder; it's about making meaningful contributions to your organization while navigating the complexities introduced by AI advancements.

Importance of Soft Skills and Communication

The workplace is changing rapidly, and *soft skills* and *communication skills* are becoming crucial for success. With automation and artificial intelligence taking over routine tasks, these skills—representing the human element—are becoming increasingly vital.

The Evolving Role of Soft Skills in the Workplace

Being technically skilled is no longer enough to ensure job security or career advancement. Employers now value candidates with strong soft skills, such as:

- **Emotional Intelligence (EQ)**: Understanding and managing your own emotions as well as those of others.

- **Adaptability**: Being flexible and open to change in a fast-paced work environment.

- **Collaboration**: Working effectively within a team to achieve common goals.

- **Conflict Resolution**: Constructively addressing disputes to maintain a harmonious workplace.

A recent study by LinkedIn revealed that 57% of leaders believe soft skills are more important than hard skills. This shift highlights the need for employees to actively develop these abilities.

Strategies for Improving Communication Abilities

Effective communication is the foundation of all professional interactions. To improve your communication skills, consider implementing the following strategies:

1. **Active Listening**:

- Pay close attention to the speaker without planning your response while they are talking.

- Provide feedback through nods or brief verbal acknowledgments like "I see" or "That makes sense."

1. **Clarity and Conciseness**:

- Aim to express your message in simple, straightforward language.

- Avoid using jargon unless it is widely understood within your industry.

1. **Non-Verbal Communication**:

- Maintain appropriate eye contact to show engagement.

- Be aware of body language; crossed arms may indicate defensiveness, while open gestures suggest receptiveness.

1. **Feedback Mechanisms**:

- Encourage and be open to receiving constructive feedback.

- Use feedback as an opportunity for personal growth rather than criticism.

Highlighting Soft Skills in Resumes and Interviews

Showcasing soft skills during the hiring process can help you stand out from other candidates. Here are some effective ways to demonstrate these competencies:

On Your Resume:

- **Professional Summary**: Include soft skills relevant to the position you're applying for in your summary statement.

  Example: "Team-oriented project manager with strong problem-solving abilities and excellent communication skills."

- **Experience Section**: Use bullet points to highlight instances where you successfully applied soft skills.

- Example:

- Led a cross-functional team of 10 members, resolving conflicts and fostering collaboration to complete projects ahead of schedule.

During Interviews:

- **Behavioral Questions**: Prepare answers that showcase your soft skills through real-life examples.

    Example: When asked about handling conflict, describe a specific situation where you mediated a dispute between colleagues and outline the positive outcome.

- **Body Language**: Demonstrate active listening during the interview by maintaining eye contact and nodding attentively.

- **Follow-Up Questions**: Show curiosity and engagement by asking insightful questions about team dynamics or company culture.

Integrating soft skills into your professional skill set is not just beneficial but essential in navigating today's complex work environments. These abilities not only enhance individual performance but also significantly contribute to organizational success.

Hands-On Training and Apprenticeships

Value of Practical Training Programs

The transition to AI-resistant jobs often necessitates a hands-on approach. Unlike theoretical knowledge, practical training programs enable individuals to apply what they've learned in real-world scenarios. This experiential learning not only solidifies theoretical concepts but also hones technical skills, making candidates more adept at tackling industry-specific challenges.

Benefits of Practical Training:

- **Skill Refinement**: Direct application of knowledge helps refine skills that are critical for job performance.

- **Industry-Relevant Experience**: Exposure to industry-standard tools and practices equips individuals with relevant experience.

- **Immediate Feedback**: Hands-on training often includes mentorship, providing immediate feedback and opportunities for improvement.

How Apprenticeships Bridge the Gap

Apprenticeships serve as a pivotal link between education and employment. They offer a structured pathway where learners can gain industry-specific skills while working alongside seasoned professionals. This form of training is especially beneficial in sectors where AI integration is minimal.

Key Advantages of Apprenticeships:

- **Real-World Experience**: Apprentices can apply their academic knowledge in practical settings, gaining invaluable industry insights.

- **Networking Opportunities**: Working with professionals provides apprentices with essential networking opportunities, fostering future career growth.

- **Employability**: Employers often prefer candidates with hands-on experience, making apprenticeships an effective way to enhance employability.

Success Stories from Apprenticeship Programs

Numerous success stories underscore the transformative power of apprenticeships. These narratives highlight how hands-on training has enabled individuals to transition into fulfilling, AI-resistant careers.

Example 1: The Tech Savvy Carpenter

John Doe started as an apprentice carpenter. With rigorous training under the guidance of experienced carpenters, John mastered the craft and eventually opened his own business. His journey exemplifies how hands-on training can turn passion into a sustainable career.

Example 2: The Healthcare Hero

Jane Smith's apprenticeship in nursing provided her with extensive clinical experience before she even completed her degree. This early exposure allowed her to excel in patient care roles immediately after graduation, demonstrating the effectiveness of practical training in healthcare fields.

Leveraging Mentorship and Coaching

Mentorship programs and **coaching relationships** are powerful tools for career transitions, especially in the context of navigating towards AI-resistant jobs. The impact of mentorship on career development is profound, often accelerating professional growth through guidance, knowledge sharing, and networking opportunities.

The Impact of Mentorship on Career Transitions

The influence of a mentor can be compared to a lighthouse guiding ships through dangerous waters. A mentor provides:

- **Expertise and Experience**: Seasoned professionals offer insights that can significantly shorten the learning curve.

- **Networking Opportunities**: Access to an established network can open doors to new job opportunities and collaborations.

- **Emotional Support**: Navigating a career transition is challenging; mentors provide encouragement and motivation.

Consider the story of Sheryl Sandberg, the COO of Facebook. She credits much of her success to mentorship from key figures in her career, highlighting how their advice helped her navigate complex corporate landscapes.

Finding a Mentor or Coach in Your Field

Locating a suitable mentor or coach requires strategic effort:
    1. **Identify Potential Mentors**: Look within your existing

network, professional groups, or industry events for individuals whose careers you admire.

2. **Leverage Professional Associations**: Joining associations relevant to your field often provides access to mentorship programs and seasoned professionals.

3. **Utilize Online Platforms**: Websites like LinkedIn allow you to connect with industry leaders who might be willing to offer guidance.

Example: John, an aspiring data scientist, found his mentor through a LinkedIn group dedicated to AI enthusiasts. This connection provided him with valuable insights into the industry and helped him land his first job.

Tips for Establishing Productive Mentorship Relationships

Creating an effective mentorship relationship involves mutual respect, clear communication, and defined goals:

- **Set Clear Objectives**: Outline what you hope to achieve from the relationship—whether it's gaining specific skills or broader career advice.

- **Regular Meetings**: Schedule consistent check-ins to discuss progress, challenges, and next steps.

- **Active Listening and Feedback**: Engage actively during discussions and be open to constructive criticism.

Practical Steps for Success:

1. **Prepare for Meetings**: Come with specific questions or topics to maximize the value of each session.

2. **Show Appreciation**: Recognize your mentor's time and effort by expressing gratitude and showing tangible progress based on their advice.

3. **Be Proactive**: Take initiative in scheduling meetings and following up on action items discussed during sessions.

Mentorship transcends simple advice-giving; it fosters a dynamic relationship where both parties learn and grow. As Maya Angelou aptly stated, "In order to be a mentor, and an effective one, one must care."

Coaching Relationships

Unlike mentorships which often develop organically over time, coaching relationships are typically more structured:

- **Goal-Oriented Approach**: Coaches help individuals set and achieve specific career goals.

- **Skill Development Focus**: Emphasis on improving particular skills or behaviors relevant to career advancement.

- **Professional Accountability Partner**: Coaches provide accountability by regularly tracking progress against set objectives.

Example: Sarah sought out a career coach when transitioning from teaching to instructional design. Through targeted coaching sessions focusing on skill development and resume building, she successfully navigated this transition within six months.

Leveraging mentorship programs and coaching relationships creates robust support systems essential for navigating complex career transitions. By strategically seeking out mentors or coaches in your field and establishing productive relationships, you unlock invaluable resources that can significantly enhance your journey toward AI-resistant roles.

Continuous Professional Development

Importance of Ongoing Education Beyond Formal Schooling

Lifelong learning is more than just a buzzword; it's a necessity in a rapidly changing job market. Traditional education provides a basic understanding, but the pace of technological advancements demands continuous professional development. This kind of ongoing education ensures that professionals remain relevant and competitive.

Lifelong learning bridges the gap between current skills and the future demands of the industry. For instance, an engineer who graduated five years ago might not have studied the latest AI algorithms now being used in their field. By engaging in continuous professional development, they can update their knowledge and remain at the forefront of innovation.

Resources for Continuous Professional Growth

A wide range of resources are available to support continuous professional growth:

- **Online Courses**: Platforms like Coursera, edX, and LinkedIn Learning offer courses on cutting-edge topics.

- **Industry Journals**: Subscribing to journals such as *Harvard Business Review* or *IEEE Spectrum* keeps professionals updated with the latest research and trends.

- **Professional Associations**: Membership in associations like IEEE or AMA provides access to workshops, conferences, and networking opportunities.

- **Webinars and Podcasts**: Engaging with webinars and podcasts by industry experts can provide insights that are both timely and relevant.

Setting Personal Development Goals

Establishing personal development goals helps create a roadmap for lifelong learning. These goals should be SMART (Specific, Measurable, Achievable, Relevant, Time-bound):

1. **Identify Skill Gaps**: Conduct a self-assessment or seek feedback from peers to identify areas for improvement.

2. **Set Clear Objectives**: Define what you aim to achieve within a specific timeframe. For example, "Complete an advanced course in machine learning within six months."

3. **Create an Action Plan**: Break down objectives into manageable steps. If your goal is to learn a new programming language, your action plan might include daily practice sessions or coding challenges.

4. **Monitor Progress**: Regularly review your progress against your goals. Adjust your plan as needed to stay on track.

5. **Celebrate Achievements**: Recognize when you've reached milestones to maintain motivation.

Real-World Examples

Consider Elon Musk's approach to continuous learning. Despite his demanding schedule, Musk dedicates time for reading and absorbing new information across various fields—from AI to space exploration. This commitment to lifelong learning has been instrumental in his ability to innovate across multiple industries.

Another compelling example is Mary Barra, CEO of General Motors. Barra emphasizes the importance of staying current with industry trends through continuous education and encourages her team to do the same. Her leadership has propelled GM into the future of autonomous and electric vehicles.

The Power of Cause-and-Effect Relationships

Engaging in continuous professional development creates a powerful feedback loop:

1. **Skill Enhancement**: As individuals acquire new skills, they become more effective in their roles.

2. **Career Advancement**: Enhanced effectiveness often leads to career progression opportunities.

3. **Increased Value**: Professionals who continually develop themselves are seen as valuable assets by their organizations.

4. **Organizational Growth**: Companies benefit from having highly skilled employees who drive innovation and efficiency.

This cause-and-effect relationship underscores why continuous professional development is not just beneficial but essential.

Hypothetical Scenario

Imagine two marketing professionals—Jane and John—who started their careers at the same time with similar qualifications. Jane prioritizes ongoing education by attending workshops and enrolling in online courses on digital marketing trends. John relies solely on his initial degree.

Over time, Jane's proactive approach enables her to implement innovative strategies that significantly boost her company's market presence—leading to her rapid promotion. John, on the other hand, struggles to keep up with industry changes and remains stagnant in his role.

This scenario illustrates how commitment to *lifelong learning* can dramatically impact career trajectories.

The Importance of Reading to Sharpen Your Mind and Critical Thinking

Reading is not just a hobby; it's a powerful workout for your brain, similar to how physical exercise benefits your body. This activity can greatly improve critical thinking skills and expand knowledge, especially in a time when jobs that cannot be replaced by AI require advanced cognitive abilities.

Enhancing Analytical Abilities

Reading activates various mental processes, encouraging the brain to analyze, interpret, and combine information.

- **Complex Problem-Solving**: Exploring different subjects—such as philosophy or science fiction—boosts the ability to solve intricate problems by introducing new ways of thinking.

- **Pattern Recognition**: Regular reading trains the mind to identify patterns and connect unrelated ideas, which is crucial for coming up with new ideas.

Broadening Knowledge Horizons

Reading broadens your understanding, exposing you to new ideas and viewpoints that are essential for remaining competitive in jobs that AI cannot replace.

- **Industry Insights**: Books and articles about industry trends offer valuable knowledge that helps professionals stay ahead of technological changes.

- **Historical Context**: Knowing about historical events provides background information for understanding current issues, leading to better decision-making.

Strengthening Communication Skills

Good communication is vital in any workplace. Reading plays a key role in improving both writing and speaking abilities.

- **Vocabulary Expansion**: Encountering different writing styles and words increases vocabulary, making it easier to express oneself.

- **Articulation of Ideas**: Reading well-crafted pieces enhances the skill of conveying complex thoughts clearly and convincingly.

Cultivating Empathy and Emotional Intelligence

Books provide insight into human experiences, nurturing empathy—a crucial quality in emotional intelligence necessary for leadership positions.

> "A reader lives a thousand lives before he dies . . . The man who never reads lives only one." — George R.R. Martin

This quote captures the life-changing impact of reading. By immersing oneself in various stories, one learns to understand others' perspectives better.

Recommended Reading Practices

To make the most out of reading, try these effective strategies:

1. **Diverse Genres**: Explore different types of books—fiction, non-fiction, biographies—to gain well-rounded insights.

2. **Critical Reading**: Approach the material with an analytical mindset by questioning what you read and considering its implications.

3. **Regular Routine**: Set aside dedicated time each day for reading. Even 30 minutes daily can lead to significant long-term benefits.

Real-Life Examples

Many successful individuals credit their achievements to a strong reading habit:

- **Warren Buffett** reportedly spends 80% of his day reading. His extensive knowledge base has been instrumental in making informed investment decisions.

- **Bill Gates** reads around 50 books a year. His reading list often includes complex subjects that fuel his innovative thinking.

Resources for Effective Reading

Using various resources can enhance your reading experience:

- **Libraries and Book Clubs**: Joining local or online book

clubs provides access to diverse materials and engaging discussions.

- **E-books and Audiobooks**: Platforms like Kindle or Audi-
ble offer flexibility for those with busy schedules.

- **Online Articles and Journals**: Websites such as Medium or
academic journals provide up-to-date information on various topics.

Reading is an essential tool for personal and professional development. It sharpens your mind, improves critical thinking skills, expands
knowledge, enhances communication abilities, and fosters empathy.
Developing a consistent reading habit can greatly contribute to success
in careers that are resistant to AI takeover. Engage actively with a variety of materials; this intellectual investment will yield immeasurable
returns.